Introduction to JavaScript: A Crash Course

An Interactive Guide to Mastering the Basics

By Laurence Lars Svekis

Dedicated to
Alexis and Sebastian
Thank you for your support

For more content and to learn more, visit

https://basescripts.com/

Source Code on GitHub

https://github.com/lsvekis/Introduction-to-JavaScript-A-Crash-Course

4

Introduction to JavaScript: A Crash Course

An Interactive Guide to Mastering the Basics

Welcome to the JavaScript Crash Course! This book is crafted to help you master the fundamentals of JavaScript through a hands-on, project-based approach. Whether you're a beginner or looking to refresh your skills, this course will guide you step by step through practical exercises, detailed explanations, and interactive coding challenges.

How to Use This Book

Step-by-Step Learning:
Each chapter is divided into clear sections that introduce a topic, explain core concepts, and then reinforce learning through practical coding exercises and quizzes. Start with the introductory sections and work your way through the examples before attempting the coding challenges.

Interactive Exercises:
Practice is key. Every section includes exercises — ranging from small coding tasks to mini projects — to help solidify your understanding. Don't hesitate to experiment with the provided examples by tweaking the code and observing the outcomes.

Quizzes and Review:
At the end of each chapter, multiple choice quizzes test your grasp of the concepts. Use these quizzes as checkpoints to assess your progress and review any areas that might need further attention.

Reference Material:
Throughout the book, you'll find coding tips, best practices, and detailed explanations of common patterns and techniques in JavaScript. These references serve as both learning aids and quick reminders as you work through your projects.

Best Practices for Learning JavaScript

1. **Code Regularly:** Consistent practice is essential. Try to code a little each day to reinforce your learning.
2. **Experiment Freely:** Modify examples and write your own code. Experimentation will help you understand how different parts of JavaScript work together.
3. **Review and Reflect:** After completing each section, review your code and the provided quizzes. Reflect on mistakes and challenges to deepen your understanding.
4. **Break Down Problems:** When facing a complex task, break it down into smaller, manageable parts. Tackle each part individually before combining them.
5. **Keep a Coding Journal:** Document your experiments, challenges, and solutions. This practice can help you track your progress and serve as a reference for future projects.
6. **Engage with the Community:** Don't hesitate to seek help from online forums, study groups, or fellow learners. Sharing your code and ideas can provide new insights and solutions.
7. **Practice Debugging:** Learning to debug is as important as writing code. Use browser developer tools to trace and fix errors.
8. **Focus on Fundamentals:** Master the core concepts — like variables, functions, and control structures — before moving on to more advanced topics.
9. **Build Projects:** Apply what you learn by building small projects. This real-world application reinforces concepts and builds confidence.

10. **Stay Curious:** JavaScript is continuously evolving. Keep learning and exploring new features, libraries, and best practices beyond this course.

This chapter is designed to set the stage for your learning experience. Use the guidelines and tips provided here as you progress through the course, and refer back to this chapter whenever you need a refresher on how to maximize your learning.

Chapter 1: Getting Started with JavaScript

In this chapter you will learn the fundamentals of JavaScript. We begin with an overview of what JavaScript is and why it matters. Then we'll set up your development environment and write your very first programs. We'll cover core concepts like variables, data types, and basic arithmetic operations through engaging, hands-on projects and plenty of coding challenges.

This chapter is divided into five sections:
- What is JavaScript?
- Setting Up Your Development Environment
- Your First JavaScript Program: "Hello, World!"
- Variables and Data Types

- Basic Operations and Expressions

Each section includes multiple coding exercises and quiz questions to help you practice and solidify your understanding.

What is JavaScript?

JavaScript is a versatile, high-level programming language primarily used to add interactivity to web pages. It runs in browsers (and on servers with platforms like Node.js), enabling you to build dynamic web applications and interactive websites. In a project-based approach, you will see how small pieces of JavaScript code can come together to create real, interactive projects.

Detailed Explanation

Dynamic and Interactive: JavaScript brings websites to life by allowing elements to respond to user actions, update content without refreshing the page, and handle events like clicks and key presses.

Ubiquitous Presence: Nearly every modern web browser supports JavaScript, and it has become the standard for front-end web development.

Beginners Friendly: The syntax is approachable and there's a wealth of tutorials, documentation, and community support available.

Coding Exercises

Exercise 1 – Document Your Understanding
Task: Create a plain text file named JavaScriptIntro.txt and write a short paragraph (4–6 sentences) explaining in your own words what JavaScript is and why it is important for web development.

Exercise 2 – Embedding a Description in HTML

Task: Create an HTML file named `about-js.html`. In the `<script>` tag, add a single-line comment that briefly describes JavaScript. For example:

```
<!-- JavaScript is a dynamic programming
language that powers interactive web
experiences. -->
<script>
  // JavaScript enables interactive elements
on websites.
</script>
```

Goal: Familiarize yourself with embedding JavaScript code within HTML.

Multiple Choice Quiz

Which of the following best describes JavaScript?
A. A style sheet language for designing web pages.
B. A programming language used to add interactivity to web pages.
C. A markup language used to structure web content.
D. A database query language.
Correct Answer: B

What is the primary purpose of JavaScript in web development?
A. To structure the content of web pages.
B. To style web pages with colors and layouts.
C. To add dynamic and interactive behavior to web pages.
D. To store data on the server.
Correct Answer: C

Where does JavaScript primarily execute?
A. On the server only.
B. Within the web browser.
C. In a standalone application without a browser.
D. In a text editor.
Correct Answer: B

Setting Up Your Development Environment

Before writing any code, you need a proper development environment. This section guides you through installing a code editor, creating your first HTML file, and accessing your browser's console.

Detailed Steps

Code Editor: Use a modern code editor like Visual Studio Code, Sublime Text, or Atom to write your code. These editors offer syntax highlighting and useful features that improve your coding workflow.

Web Browser: Any modern browser (Chrome, Firefox, Edge) will work. We recommend Google Chrome for its robust developer tools.

Browser Console: The browser console is your real-time output window for JavaScript. To open it in Chrome, press Ctrl+Shift+J (or Cmd+Option+J on a Mac).

Coding Exercises

Exercise 3 – Create Your First HTML File

Task: Create a file named `index.html` with the following structure:

```
<!DOCTYPE html>
<html lang="en">
<head>
  <meta charset="UTF-8">
  <title>JavaScript Environment Setup</title>
</head>
<body>
  <h1>Welcome to JavaScript!</h1>
  <script>
    // Your JavaScript code will go here.
    console.log("Environment is set up!");
  </script>
</body>
</html>
```

Goal: Open this file in your web browser and check the console for the message.

Exercise 4 – Manipulate the DOM

Task: In the same `index.html`, add a `<div>` with an `id` of "message". Then, write JavaScript code to change its text content:

```
<div id="message">Original Text</div>
<script>

document.getElementById("message").textContent
= "Text updated by JavaScript!";
```

12

```
</script>
```

Goal: Learn to access and manipulate HTML elements with JavaScript.

Exercise 5 – Verify Your Console Output

Task: Add another `console.log()` statement to print a custom message. For example:

```
console.log("This is a custom debug
message.");
```

Goal: Reinforce how to view outputs in the browser console.

Multiple Choice Quiz

Which tool is primarily used to write and edit JavaScript code?
A. Spreadsheet software
B. Code Editor
C. Word Processor
D. Photo Editor
Correct Answer: B

How do you open the browser console in Google Chrome?
A. Press F5
B. Press Ctrl+Shift+J (or Cmd+Option+J on Mac)
C. Right-click and select "Inspect" then choose the "Elements" tab
D. The console opens automatically with every webpage
Correct Answer: B

What file extension is used for HTML files?
A. .js
B. .html
C. .css
D. .txt
Correct Answer: B

Your First JavaScript Program: "Hello, World!"

A classic starting point for every programmer is the "Hello, World!" program. This simple script outputs text to the browser console, ensuring that your environment is working correctly.

Detailed Explanation

console.log(): This function writes a message to the browser's console, helping you debug and verify that your code runs as expected.
String Literals: Text enclosed in quotes (either single or double) that JavaScript interprets as a string.

Coding Exercises
Exercise 6 – Basic Hello, World!
Task: In your index.html, inside the <script> tag, write:
```
console.log("Hello, World!");
```
Goal: See "Hello, World!" printed in the console.
Exercise 7 – Personalized Greeting
Task: Modify the previous code to output a personalized greeting. For example:

```
console.log("Hello, Alex!");
```
Goal: Learn how to customize output messages.
Exercise 8 – String Concatenation
Task: Write code that concatenates two strings and outputs the result:

```
let part1 = "Hello";
let part2 = "World";
console.log(part1 + ", " + part2 + "!");
```

Goal: Understand how to join strings together.

Multiple Choice Quiz

What function is used to log messages to the browser console?
A. print()
B. console.log()
C. alert()
D. document.write()
Correct Answer: B

What will be the output of console.log("Hello, World!");?
A. Nothing, it will cause an error.
B. The text "Hello, World!" will appear in the console.
C. A popup window with "Hello, World!".
D. It will write "Hello, World!" to the HTML page.
Correct Answer: B

Which of the following is a string literal in JavaScript?
A. hello
B. "hello"
C. 123
D. true
Correct Answer: B

Variables and Data Types

Variables are containers for storing data. JavaScript supports various data types such as strings, numbers, and booleans. You declare variables using keywords like `let` and `const`.

Detailed Explanation

let vs. const:
Use let for variables that may change later.
Use const for values that should not be reassigned.

Data Types:
String: Text enclosed in quotes, e.g., "Hello".

Number: Numeric values, e.g., 42 or 3.14.

Boolean: Logical values, either true or false.

Coding Exercises
Exercise 9 – Declare and Inspect Variables
Task: Declare variables of different types and use the `typeof` operator to log their types:

```
let greeting = "Hello, JavaScript!";
let year = 2025;
let isFun = true;
console.log(typeof greeting); // Expected
output: string
console.log(typeof year);      // Expected
output: number
console.log(typeof isFun);     // Expected
output: boolean
```

Goal: Learn how to declare variables and inspect their data types.

Exercise 10 – let vs. const
Task:

Declare a variable using let and assign it a value.

Change its value and log it to the console.

Declare another variable using const and attempt to reassign it (observe the error in your console).

```
let mutableVar = "I can change";
console.log(mutableVar);
mutableVar = "I have changed!";
console.log(mutableVar);
const immutableVar = "I cannot change";
console.log(immutableVar);
// Uncommenting the next line should cause an
error:
// immutableVar = "Trying to change";
```

Goal: Understand the difference in behavior between let and const.

Exercise 11 – Using Template Literals

Task: Create variables for your name and age, then use a template literal to log a sentence:

```
let myName = "Alex";
let myAge = 25;
console.log(`My name is ${myName} and I am
${myAge} years old.`);
```

Goal: Practice using template literals to embed variables in strings.

Multiple Choice Quiz

Which of the following is a correct way to declare a variable in modern JavaScript?

A. let x = 10;

B. var x = 10;

C. x = 10;

D. const x = 10;

Correct Answers: A and D

What will typeof 42 return?

A. "string"

B. "number"

C. "boolean"

D. "object"

Correct Answer: B

Which keyword is used to declare a variable whose value should not change?

A. let

B. var

C. const

D. static

Correct Answer: C

What does the operator typeof do in JavaScript?

A. Converts a value to a string.

B. Returns the data type of a variable.

C. Changes the data type of a variable.

D. Compares two variables for equality.

Correct Answer: B

Basic Operations and Expressions

JavaScript supports a variety of arithmetic operators that let you perform calculations. This section introduces you to addition, subtraction, multiplication, division, and the modulo operator.

Detailed Explanation

Arithmetic Operators:
Addition (+)
Subtraction (-)
Multiplication (*)

Division (/)

Modulo (%) returns the remainder after division.
Expressions: Combinations of values and operators that are evaluated to produce a result.

Coding Exercises
Exercise 12 – Arithmetic Operations
Task: Write code that performs basic arithmetic operations on two numbers and logs the results:

```
let a = 10;
let b = 5;
console.log("Sum:", a + b);              // 15
console.log("Difference:", a - b);       // 5
console.log("Product:", a * b);          // 50
console.log("Quotient:", a / b);         // 2
```

Goal: Get comfortable using arithmetic operators.
Exercise 13 – Using the Modulo Operator
Task: Write code to calculate the remainder when 10 is divided by 3:

```
let remainder = 10 % 3;
```

```
console.log("Remainder:", remainder); //
Expected output: 1
```

Goal: Understand the modulo operator.

Exercise 14 – Calculate the Area of a Rectangle

Task: Declare two variables for width and height, then compute and log the area:

```
let width = 8;
let height = 4;
let area = width * height;
console.log("Area of the rectangle:", area);
```

Goal: Apply arithmetic operations to solve a real-world problem.

Exercise 15 – Average of Numbers

Task: Write a program that calculates the average of three numbers:

```
let num1 = 10;
let num2 = 20;
let num3 = 30;
let average = (num1 + num2 + num3) / 3;
console.log("Average:", average);
```

Goal: Practice combining arithmetic operations in an expression.

Multiple Choice Quiz

Which operator is used for multiplication in JavaScript?
A. x
B. *
C. multiply
D. %
Correct Answer: B

What is the output of the following code?

```
console.log(10 % 3);
```

A. 1
B. 3
C. 0
D. 10
Correct Answer: A

Which of the following is NOT an arithmetic operator in JavaScript?
A. +
B. -
C. **
D. &&
Correct Answer: D

If a = 10 and b = 5, what is the value of a - b?
A. 15
B. 5
C. -5
D. 50
Correct Answer: B

Summary & Next Steps

In this chapter, you have learned:
What JavaScript is and why it is a key tool for creating interactive web pages.

How to set up your development environment with a modern code editor and browser console.

How to write your first JavaScript program, starting with the classic "Hello, World!" example.

How to declare and use variables with let and const, and inspect their data types.
How to perform basic arithmetic operations and combine expressions to solve simple problems.

Final Project for Chapter 1

Using everything you've learned, complete the following project:
Create an HTML file (e.g., project1.html) that includes:

A heading welcoming the user.

Several <script> blocks that:
Log a personalized greeting.
Demonstrate string concatenation.

Declare variables of different types and print their types.

Perform arithmetic operations (including addition, subtraction, multiplication, division, and modulo).
Calculate and display the area of a rectangle and the average of three numbers.
Experiment by modifying variable values and adding new console.log() statements to see how the output changes.

This project will serve as a stepping stone for more complex projects in the coming chapters.

By completing these detailed exercises and quizzes, you have taken your first steps into the world of JavaScript. As you progress through this course, you will build on these fundamentals with functions, control structures, DOM manipulation, and more advanced topics—all through practical, project-based learning.

Chapter 2: Control Structures and Functions

Programming is not just about writing code—it's about making decisions and repeating tasks efficiently. In this chapter, you will learn:

- Conditional Statements: How to let your program make decisions using if, else if, else, and switch statements.
- Looping Structures: How to perform repetitive tasks using loops like for, while, and do-while.
- Functions: How to encapsulate code into reusable blocks, pass data into functions via parameters, and return values.

- We'll also combine these concepts in a mini project to give you a taste of real-world programming.

Section 1: Conditional Statements

Conditional statements allow your code to choose different paths based on whether a condition is true or false.

Detailed Explanation

if Statement: Executes a block of code if a condition is true.
if...else Statement: Executes one block if the condition is true and another if it's false.
if...else if...else Chain: Evaluates multiple conditions in sequence.
switch Statement: Chooses a block of code to execute based on different possible values of a variable.

Code Examples

Example 1 – if / else:
```
let score = 85;
if (score >= 90) {
  console.log("Grade: A");
} else if (score >= 80) {
  console.log("Grade: B");
} else {
  console.log("Grade: C or below");
}
```

Example 2 – switch:

```javascript
let day = "Tuesday";
switch (day) {
  case "Monday":
    console.log("Start of the work week.");
    break;
  case "Tuesday":
    console.log("Second day of the week.");
    break;
  case "Friday":
    console.log("End of the work week.");
    break;
  default:
    console.log("Midweek days or weekend.");
}
```

Coding Exercises
Exercise 1 – Basic If Statement
Task: Write an **if** statement that checks if a number stored in a variable num is positive. If it is, log "**Positive**" to the console.

```javascript
let num = 7;
if (num > 0) {
  console.log("Positive");
}
```

Exercise 2 – If...Else Chain
Task: Write a program that checks a variable temperature and logs:
"Hot" if above 30

"Warm" if between 20 and 30

"Cold" if below 20

```javascript
let temperature = 25;
if (temperature > 30) {
```

```
  console.log("Hot");
} else if (temperature >= 20) {
  console.log("Warm");
} else {
  console.log("Cold");
}
```

Exercise 3 – Switch Statement

Task: Create a variable `fruit` with a value of your choice (e.g., "apple", "banana", etc.) and use a switch statement to log a custom message for at least three different fruits. Provide a default message for any other fruit.

```
let fruit = "banana";
switch (fruit) {
  case "apple":
    console.log("An apple a day keeps the
doctor away.");
    break;
  case "banana":
    console.log("Bananas are rich in
potassium.");
    break;
  case "orange":
    console.log("Oranges are full of vitamin
C.");
    break;
  default:
    console.log("Enjoy your fruit!");
}
```

Exercise 4 – Nested Conditionals

Task: Write code that checks if a user is logged in (boolean variable `isLoggedIn`). If they are, check if their role (variable `role`) is "admin"; if so, log "Welcome, Admin", otherwise log "Welcome, User". If not logged in, log "Please log in".

```
let isLoggedIn = true;
let role = "admin";
if (isLoggedIn) {
  if (role === "admin") {
    console.log("Welcome, Admin");
  } else {
    console.log("Welcome, User");
  }
} else {
  console.log("Please log in");
}
```

Exercise 5 – Ternary Operator

Task: Rewrite a simple if-else condition using the ternary operator. For a variable `age`, log "Adult" if `age` is 18 or above, otherwise log "Minor".

```
let age = 16;
console.log(age >= 18 ? "Adult" : "Minor");
```

Multiple Choice Quiz – Conditionals

What does an if statement do in JavaScript?
A. Repeats a block of code
B. Executes code based on a condition
C. Declares a variable
D. Imports modules
Correct Answer: B

Which keyword is used to provide an alternative block of code if an if condition is false?
A. else
B. then
C. default
D. case
Correct Answer: A

In a switch statement, what does the break keyword do?
A. Exits the entire program
B. Stops checking further cases
C. Continues to the next case
D. Skips the default case
Correct Answer: B
Which of the following is a correct syntax for an if statement?
A. if num > 0 { console.log("Positive"); }
B. if (num > 0) console.log("Positive");
C. if (num > 0) { console.log("Positive") }
D. Both B and C
Correct Answer: D
How can you write a one-line if-else statement?
A. Using a ternary operator
B. Using a switch statement
C. Using a loop
D. It is not possible
Correct Answer: A

Section 2: Looping Structures

Loops enable your program to execute a block of code repeatedly. Here, you'll learn about for, while, and do-while loops.

Detailed Explanation

For Loop: Ideal when the number of iterations is known.
While Loop: Executes as long as the condition is true.

Do-While Loop: Executes at least once before checking the condition.

Code Examples

Example 1 – For Loop:
```
for (let i = 1; i <= 5; i++) {
   console.log("Iteration:", i);
}
```

Example 2 – While Loop:
```
let count = 1;
while (count <= 5) {
   console.log("Count is:", count);
   count++;
}
```

Example 3 – Do-While Loop:
```
let j = 1;
do {
   console.log("j =", j);
   j++;
} while (j <= 5);
```

Coding Exercises
Exercise 6 – Counting with a For Loop
Task: Write a for loop that logs the numbers from 1 to 10.

```
for (let i = 1; i <= 10; i++) {
   console.log(i);
}
```
Exercise 7 – Sum of Array Elements
Task: Given an array of numbers, use a for loop to compute and log the sum of its elements.

```
let numbers = [5, 10, 15, 20];
let sum = 0;
for (let i = 0; i < numbers.length; i++) {
```

```
    sum += numbers[i];
}
console.log("Sum:", sum);
```

Exercise 8 – While Loop Practice

Task: Using a while loop, print the even numbers between 2 and 20.

```
let number = 2;
while (number <= 20) {
   if (number % 2 === 0) {
      console.log(number);
   }
   number++;
}
```

Exercise 9 – Do-While Loop Minimum

Task: Use a do-while loop to print "Hello" at least once, even if the condition is initially false. (Hint: Set the condition to false after the first iteration.)

```
let x = 10;
do {
   console.log("Hello");
   x = 0; // Change condition to false after
first iteration
} while (x > 10);
```

Multiple Choice Quiz – Loops

Which loop is most appropriate when you know exactly how many times you want to iterate?
A. While loop
B. Do-while loop
C. For loop
D. Infinite loop
Correct Answer: C

What is the key difference between a while loop and a do-while loop?

A. A while loop runs at least once, but a do-while loop may not run at all.

B. A do-while loop runs at least once, while a while loop may not run if the condition is false initially.

C. There is no difference.

D. The do-while loop requires a counter variable.

Correct Answer: B

How do you increment a counter variable inside a for loop?

A. i++

B. i--

C. i += 2

D. Both A and C (depending on the desired step)

Correct Answer: D

Section 3: Functions

Functions are reusable blocks of code that perform a specific task. They help keep your code organized and avoid repetition.

Detailed Explanation

Function Declaration: A standard way to create functions.
Function Expression: Functions can also be assigned to variables.

Arrow Functions: A concise syntax introduced in ES6.

Parameters and Return Values: Functions can take inputs (parameters) and return outputs.

Code Examples

Example 1 – Function Declaration:

```
function greet(name) {
    return `Hello, ${name}!`;
}
```

```
console.log(greet("Alice"));
```

Example 2 – Function Expression:
```
const add = function(a, b) {
   return a + b;
};
console.log("Sum:", add(5, 3));
```

Example 3 – Arrow Function:
```
const multiply = (x, y) => x * y;
console.log("Product:", multiply(4, 6));
```

Coding Exercises
Exercise 10 – Simple Function
Task: Write a function called square that takes a number as a parameter and returns its square. Call the function and log the result.

```
function square(num) {
   return num * num;
}
console.log("Square of 5:", square(5));
```
Exercise 11 – Function with Multiple Parameters
Task: Create a function calculateArea that accepts width and height as parameters and returns the area of a rectangle. Log the result.

```
function calculateArea(width, height) {
   return width * height;
}
console.log("Area:", calculateArea(8, 5));
```
Exercise 12 – Arrow Function Practice
Task: Convert the following function expression into an arrow function:

```
// Original function expression
const subtract = function(a, b) {
```

```
  return a - b;
};
// Convert to arrow function:
const subtractArrow = (a, b) => a - b;
console.log("Difference:", subtractArrow(10,
3));
```

Exercise 13 – Function with Conditionals

Task: Write a function checkNumber that accepts a number and returns:

"Positive" if the number is greater than zero

"Negative" if it is less than zero

"Zero" if it equals zero

```
function checkNumber(num) {
  if (num > 0) {
    return "Positive";
  } else if (num < 0) {
    return "Negative";
  } else {
    return "Zero";
  }
}
console.log("Check 10:", checkNumber(10));
console.log("Check -5:", checkNumber(-5));
console.log("Check 0:", checkNumber(0));
```

Section 4: Combining Concepts – Mini Project

Now, let's put control structures and functions together in a small project. You'll create a basic program that simulates a simple quiz game.

Project Overview

Create a program that:
Asks the user (via pre-set variables) a simple math question.

Uses a function to check the answer.

Uses conditionals to determine if the answer is correct.

Uses a loop to allow the user to try up to 3 times before ending the game.

Code Example

```
// Define the correct answer
const correctAnswer = 12;
// Function to check the answer
function checkAnswer(userAnswer) {
   if (userAnswer === correctAnswer) {
     return true;
   }
   return false;
}
// Simulated user attempts (in a real
scenario, you might use prompt() to get input)
const userAttempts = [10, 12, 15];
let attempt = 0;
let isCorrect = false;
while (attempt < userAttempts.length &&
!isCorrect) {
   const answer = userAttempts[attempt];
   console.log(`Attempt ${attempt + 1}: User
answered ${answer}`);
   if (checkAnswer(answer)) {
     console.log("Correct answer! You win!");
     isCorrect = true;
   } else {
     console.log("Incorrect answer. Try
again!");
   }
   attempt++;
}
if (!isCorrect) {
```

```
    console.log("Game over. Better luck next
time!");
}
```

Coding Exercise
Exercise 14 – Enhance the Quiz Game
Task: Modify the quiz game so that it also tells the user if their answer was too high or too low. (Hint: Update the checkAnswer function or add a new function for hints.)

```
function checkAnswerWithHint(userAnswer) {
  if (userAnswer === correctAnswer) {
    return { correct: true, hint: "Correct!"
};
  } else if (userAnswer < correctAnswer) {
    return { correct: false, hint: "Too low!"
};
  } else {
    return { correct: false, hint: "Too high!"
};
  }
}
attempt = 0;
isCorrect = false;
while (attempt < userAttempts.length &&
!isCorrect) {
  const answer = userAttempts[attempt];
  const result = checkAnswerWithHint(answer);
  console.log(`Attempt ${attempt + 1}: User
answered ${answer}. ${result.hint}`);
  if (result.correct) {
    isCorrect = true;
  }
  attempt++;
}
if (!isCorrect) {
```

```
    console.log("Game over. Better luck next
time!");
}
```

Exercise 15 – Create a Reusable Function

Task: Write a function `repeatMessage` that accepts two parameters: a message (string) and a count (number). The function should log the message to the console the specified number of times.

```
function repeatMessage(message, count) {
    for (let i = 0; i < count; i++) {
        console.log(message);
    }
}
repeatMessage("Keep practicing!", 3);
```

Multiple Choice Quiz – Functions & Combined Concepts

What is the purpose of a function in JavaScript?
A. To store data permanently
B. To encapsulate reusable code
C. To loop through arrays
D. To style web pages
Correct Answer: B
Which syntax correctly defines an arrow function that multiplies two numbers?
A. const multiply = (a, b) => a * b;
B. function multiply(a, b) => a * b;
C. const multiply = (a, b) { return a * b; };
D. multiply(a, b) => a * b;
Correct Answer: A

How do you call a function named greet with the argument "Bob"?
A. greet("Bob")
B. greet: "Bob"
C. call greet("Bob")
D. greet->"Bob"
Correct Answer: A

In the context of functions, what is a parameter?
A. The value returned by a function
B. A variable used to store the result of a function
C. A placeholder for values passed into a function
D. A built-in JavaScript keyword
Correct Answer: C

Which loop guarantees that the code block will execute at least once?
A. for loop
B. while loop
C. do-while loop
D. None of the above
Correct Answer: C

What is returned by the following function call?

```
function add(a, b) {
    return a + b;
}
console.log(add(4, 6));
```

A. "4,6"
B. 10
C. "10"
D. undefined
Correct Answer: B

When using a switch statement, if no case matches, which block of code is executed?
A. The first case
B. The last case
C. The default block
D. Nothing is executed
Correct Answer: C

Recap & Next Steps

In this chapter, you learned to:

Use conditional statements to let your program decide which code to run.

Implement loops for repeating tasks with for, while, and do-while loops.
Write functions to package and reuse code, including function declarations, expressions, and arrow functions.
Combine these concepts in a mini project that simulates a simple quiz game, incorporating both conditionals and loops.

Final Mini Project Challenge

As a final challenge for this chapter, try building a small interactive quiz game using your own set of questions and answers. Use functions to handle user input (or simulated input), conditional statements to check answers, and loops to allow multiple attempts. Experiment with additional features such as score tracking or randomized questions to enhance the project further.

By working through these detailed examples, coding exercises, and quizzes, you have strengthened your understanding of control structures and functions in JavaScript. These are the building blocks for creating more complex and dynamic projects. In the next chapter, we will dive deeper into arrays, objects, and more advanced data structures — continuing our journey toward mastering Vanilla JavaScript.

Chapter 3: Arrays, Objects, and Data Structures

Data is at the heart of any program. In JavaScript, arrays and objects are the building blocks for organizing and working with data. This chapter is organized into the following sections:

- Introduction to Arrays
- Introduction to Objects
- Combining Arrays and Objects
- Mini Project: Building an Address Book
- Comprehensive Quiz

Each section features numerous code examples, practical coding tips, a variety of exercises, and an abundance of multiple choice questions to deepen your understanding.

Introduction to Arrays

Arrays are ordered collections of values that can store multiple items in a single variable. They are versatile and come with a host of built-in methods that simplify tasks like adding, removing, and iterating over items.

Detailed Explanation

Creating Arrays: Arrays can be created using square brackets [] or the Array constructor.
Indexing: Array elements are zero-indexed (the first element is at index 0).

Common Methods: push(), pop(), shift(), unshift(), splice(), slice(), and forEach().
Iteration: Use loops (such as for, for...of, or forEach) to process each element.

Coding Tips

Tip 1: When iterating over an array, always check the length property to avoid out-of-bounds errors.

Tip 2: Use array methods like map(), filter(), and reduce() for cleaner, functional-style code.

Tip 3: Prefer for...of loops when you need to directly access each element.

Code Examples

Example 1 – Creating and Accessing an Array:
```
let fruits = ["apple", "banana", "cherry"];
console.log("First fruit:", fruits[0]); //
Output: apple
console.log("Total fruits:", fruits.length);
// Output: 3
```

Example 2 – Using Array Methods:
```
// Adding an element at the end
fruits.push("date");
console.log("After push:", fruits);
// Removing the first element
let removedFruit = fruits.shift();
console.log("Removed fruit:", removedFruit);
console.log("After shift:", fruits);
```

Example 3 – Iterating over an Array:

```
fruits.forEach((fruit, index) => {
  console.log(`Fruit ${index + 1}: ${fruit}`);
});
```

Coding Exercises: Arrays

Exercise 1 – Create an Array of Colors

Task: Create an array called `colors` that contains at least five color names. Log the array and its length.

```
let colors = ["red", "green", "blue",
"yellow", "purple"];
console.log(colors);
console.log("Total colors:", colors.length);
```

Exercise 2 – Modify Array Elements

Task: Create an array `numbers` with the values `[10, 20, 30, 40, 50]`. Change the third element to 35 and log the updated array.

```
let numbers = [10, 20, 30, 40, 50];
numbers[2] = 35;
console.log("Updated numbers:", numbers);
```

Exercise 3 – Using push() and pop()

Task: Create an array `animals` and add three animal names using `push()`. Then, remove the last element using `pop()` and log the resulting array.

```
let animals = [];
animals.push("dog");
animals.push("cat");
animals.push("rabbit");
console.log("Animals after push:", animals);
animals.pop();
console.log("Animals after pop:", animals);
```

Exercise 4 – Using splice() to Remove an Element

Task: Given an array `cities = ["New York", "Los Angeles", "Chicago", "Houston"]`, remove `"Chicago"` using `splice()` and log the updated array.

```
let cities = ["New York", "Los Angeles",
"Chicago", "Houston"];
let index = cities.indexOf("Chicago");
if (index !== -1) {
  cities.splice(index, 1);
}
console.log("Cities after removal:", cities);
```

Exercise 5 – Filtering an Array

Task: Create an array `scores = [45, 82, 68, 90, 55]` and use the `filter()` method to create a new array with scores greater than 70.

```
let scores = [45, 82, 68, 90, 55];
let highScores = scores.filter(score => score
> 70);
console.log("High scores:", highScores);
```

Exercise 6 – Mapping an Array

Task: Use the `map()` method on an array `nums = [1, 2, 3, 4, 5]` to create a new array that contains the square of each number.

```
let nums = [1, 2, 3, 4, 5];
let squares = nums.map(num => num * num);
console.log("Squares:", squares);
```

Multiple Choice Quiz – Arrays

What is the index of the first element in a JavaScript array?

A. 0
B. 1
C. -1
D. It depends on the array

Correct Answer: A

Which method adds an element to the end of an array?
A. pop()
B. push()
C. shift()
D. unshift()
Correct Answer: B

What does the length property of an array return?
A. The number of elements in the array
B. The index of the last element
C. The total memory allocated
D. The sum of all elements
Correct Answer: A

How can you remove the first element from an array?
A. array.pop()
B. array.shift()
C. array.unshift()
D. array.slice()
Correct Answer: B

Which array method would you use to create a new array containing only elements that pass a test?
A. forEach()
B. filter()
C. map()
D. reduce()
Correct Answer: B

What will be the output of the following code?
```
let arr = [2, 4, 6];
arr.push(8);
console.log(arr.length);
```
A. 3
B. 4
C. 5
D. 6
Correct Answer: B

Which method can be used to iterate over each element in an array?
A. forEach()
B. map()
C. Both A and B
D. None of the above
Correct Answer: C

Introduction to Objects

Objects in JavaScript are collections of key-value pairs. They allow you to model complex data and real-world entities by grouping related data and functions (called methods) together.

Detailed Explanation
Creating Objects: Objects are defined using curly braces {} with key-value pairs.
Accessing Properties: Use dot notation (object.property) or bracket notation (object["property"]).

Modifying Objects: You can add, update, or remove properties at any time.
Methods: Functions defined inside objects that operate on the object's data.

Coding Tips
Tip 1: Use descriptive property names to make your objects more understandable.
Tip 2: When using bracket notation, property names should be strings.
Tip 3: Use object destructuring to extract values from an object for cleaner code.

Code Examples

Example 1 – Creating an Object:
```
let person = {
```

```
    firstName: "Jane",
    lastName: "Doe",
    age: 28
};
console.log("Person:", person);
```

Example 2 – Accessing and Modifying Properties:
```
console.log("First Name:", person.firstName);
person.age = 29; // Update the age
person["city"] = "New York"; // Add a new
property
console.log("Updated Person:", person);
```

Example 3 – Adding a Method:
```
let calculator = {
    add: function(a, b) {
        return a + b;
    }
};
console.log("Calculator Add:",
calculator.add(5, 7));
```

Coding Exercises: Objects
Exercise 7 – Create a Book Object
Task: Create an object book with properties for title,
author, and pages. Log the object and then print each
property individually.
```
let book = {
    title: "JavaScript Essentials",
    author: "Alex Developer",
    pages: 250
};
console.log(book);
console.log("Title:", book.title);
console.log("Author:", book.author);
console.log("Pages:", book.pages);
```

Exercise 8 – Update Object Properties

Task: Create an object student with properties name and grade. Update the grade property and add a new property school.

```
let student = {
  name: "Sam",
  grade: "B"
};
student.grade = "A";
student.school = "Central High";
console.log("Updated Student:", student);
```

Exercise 9 – Nested Objects

Task: Create an object company that has a property name and a nested object address with street, city, and zipcode. Log the entire object and then the city.

```
let company = {
  name: "Tech Solutions",
  address: {
    street: "123 Innovation Drive",
    city: "Silicon Valley",
    zipcode: "94043"
  }
};
console.log(company);
console.log("Company City:",
company.address.city);
```

Exercise 10 – Object Destructuring

Task: Given the object:

```
let user = {
  username: "coder123",
  email: "coder@example.com",
  active: true
};
```

Use object destructuring to extract username and active into variables and log them.

```
let { username, active } = user;
```

```
console.log("Username:", username);
console.log("Active Status:", active);
```
Exercise 11 – Looping through Object Properties

Task: Create an object car with properties like make, model, and year. Use a for...in loop to log each property and its value.

```
let car = {
  make: "Toyota",
  model: "Corolla",
  year: 2020
};
for (let key in car) {
  console.log(`${key}: ${car[key]}`);
}
```

Multiple Choice Quiz – Objects

How do you define an object in JavaScript?
A. Using square brackets []
B. Using curly braces {}
C. Using parentheses ()
D. Using angle brackets <>
Correct Answer: B

Which notation is used to access the property name of an object person?
A. person->name
B. person(name)
C. person.name
D. person[name]
Correct Answer: C
(Note: person["name"] is also correct.)
What is the output of the following code?
```
let obj = { a: 10, b: 20 };
console.log(obj.a + obj.b);
```

A. "10 20"
B. 30
C. "1020"
D. undefined
Correct Answer: B
How do you add a new property color with the value "red" to an object item?
A. item.color = "red";
B. item["color"] = "red";
C. Both A and B
D. None of the above
Correct Answer: C

Which loop is typically used to iterate over the properties of an object?
A. for loop
B. while loop
C. for...in loop
D. for...of loop
Correct Answer: C

Combining Arrays and Objects

Often, you will store objects inside arrays or have objects that contain arrays. This combination allows you to manage collections of complex data.

Detailed Explanation
Arrays of Objects: Ideal for storing lists of similar items (e.g., a list of students or products).

Objects with Array Properties: Useful for representing entities that have multiple related values.

Code Examples

Example 1 – Array of Objects:
```
let students = [
```

```
  { name: "Alice", grade: 90 },
  { name: "Bob", grade: 82 },
  { name: "Charlie", grade: 88 }
];
students.forEach(student => {
  console.log(`${student.name} scored
${student.grade}`);
});
```

Example 2 – Object with an Array Property:
```
let classroom = {
  teacher: "Mrs. Smith",
  students: ["Alice", "Bob", "Charlie",
"Diana"]
};
console.log("Teacher:", classroom.teacher);
console.log("Students:",
classroom.students.join(", "));
```

Coding Exercises: Combining Arrays and Objects
Exercise 12 – List of Products
Task: Create an array called products that contains at least three objects. Each object should have properties name, price, and inStock (a boolean). Log each product's details.
```
let products = [
  { name: "Laptop", price: 999.99, inStock:
true },
  { name: "Smartphone", price: 499.99,
inStock: false },
  { name: "Tablet", price: 299.99, inStock:
true }
];
products.forEach(product => {
  console.log(`Product: ${product.name},
Price: $${product.price}, In Stock:
${product.inStock}`);
```

```
});
```
Exercise 13 – Filter Objects in an Array

Task: Given the `products` array from the previous exercise, use the `filter()` method to create a new array that only contains products that are in stock.
```
let availableProducts =
products.filter(product => product.inStock);
console.log("Available Products:",
availableProducts);
```
Exercise 14 – Update Object Inside an Array

Task: Update the price of the "Smartphone" in the `products` array to `449.99` using a loop, and then log the updated array.
```
products.forEach(product => {
  if (product.name === "Smartphone") {
    product.price = 449.99;
  }
});
console.log("Updated Products:", products);
```

Mini Project: Building an Address Book

In this mini project, you will create a simple address book that uses arrays and objects to store contact information. This project combines everything you've learned so far.

Project Overview
Objective: Build an address book that stores contacts as objects within an array.

Data: Each contact should include properties like name, phone, email, and optionally address.

Functionality: Write functions to add a contact, display all contacts, and search for a contact by name.

Code Example
```
// Define the array to hold contacts
let addressBook = [];
```

```javascript
// Function to add a new contact
function addContact(name, phone, email,
address) {
  let contact = { name, phone, email, address
};
  addressBook.push(contact);
}
// Function to display all contacts
function displayContacts() {
  console.log("Address Book:");
  addressBook.forEach((contact, index) => {
    console.log(`${index + 1}. ${contact.name}
- Phone: ${contact.phone}, Email:
${contact.email}`);
  });
}
// Function to search for a contact by name
function searchContact(name) {
  return addressBook.filter(contact =>
contact.name.toLowerCase() ===
name.toLowerCase());
}
// Adding sample contacts
addContact("Alice Johnson", "555-1234",
"alice@example.com", "123 Maple St");
addContact("Bob Smith", "555-5678",
"bob@example.com", "456 Oak Ave");
// Display all contacts
displayContacts();
// Searching for a contact
let results = searchContact("Alice Johnson");
console.log("Search Results:", results);
```

Coding Exercise: Mini Project Enhancement

Exercise 15 – Enhance the Address Book
Task:

Add a function removeContact(name) that removes a contact by name.
Test the function by removing a contact and then displaying the updated address book.

```
function removeContact(name) {
  addressBook = addressBook.filter(contact =>
contact.name.toLowerCase() !==
name.toLowerCase());
}
// Remove Bob Smith and display the updated
address book
removeContact("Bob Smith");
displayContacts();
```

Comprehensive Quiz

Test your overall understanding of arrays, objects, and data structures with the following multiple choice questions:

Which of the following correctly creates an empty array?
A. let arr = {};
B. let arr = [];
C. let arr = ();
D. let arr = new Array();
Correct Answers: B and D

What does the push() method do to an array?
A. Removes the last element
B. Adds a new element to the beginning
C. Adds a new element to the end
D. Reverses the array
Correct Answer: C

How do you access the value of the property age from an object user?
A. user.age
B. user["age"]
C. Both A and B
D. Neither A nor B
Correct Answer: C

Which array method returns a new array with elements that pass a given test?
A. forEach()
B. filter()
C. map()
D. reduce()
Correct Answer: B

What is the purpose of the for...in loop?
A. To iterate over array elements
B. To iterate over object properties
C. To iterate over numbers
D. To iterate over strings
Correct Answer: B

What will be the output of the following code snippet?
```
let arr = [1, 2, 3];
arr.unshift(0);
console.log(arr[0]);
```
A. 0
B. 1
C. Undefined
D. 3
Correct Answer: A

Which of the following is a benefit of using objects in JavaScript?
A. They help in organizing related data and functionality
B. They allow for easy sorting of data
C. They are used only for storing numbers
D. They eliminate the need for functions
Correct Answer: A

How can you remove a property from an object obj with key keyName?
A. delete obj.keyName;
B. obj.remove(keyName);
C. obj.pop(keyName);
D. remove obj.keyName;
Correct Answer: A

Recap & Next Steps

In this chapter, you learned to:
Create and manipulate arrays, including using various built-in methods.
Define and work with objects to represent complex data.

Combine arrays and objects for managing collections of structured data.
Build a mini project (an address book) to put these concepts into practice.

Final Coding Tip

Always comment your code and test each part separately. This practice not only makes your code easier to understand but also simplifies debugging as your projects grow in complexity.

By completing the exercises and quizzes in this chapter, you have built a strong foundation in handling data with arrays and objects. In the next chapter, we'll explore more advanced topics such as higher-order functions, asynchronous programming, and working with the DOM.

Chapter 4: DOM Manipulation and Event Handling

The Document Object Model (DOM) is the structured representation of an HTML document. Using JavaScript, you can access, modify, and update the elements on a page to create dynamic, interactive web experiences. In this chapter, you will learn to:

- Access and modify DOM elements using various selectors and methods.
- Manipulate HTML content and CSS styles dynamically.
- Add event listeners to handle user interactions.
- Implement a mini project that brings together your DOM manipulation and event handling skills.

Section 1: Introduction to the DOM

The DOM represents the structure of your HTML document as a tree of objects. Each HTML element becomes a node in this tree, and JavaScript can be used to traverse and manipulate these nodes.

Detailed Explanation

DOM Tree: The HTML document is modeled as a tree structure with elements as nodes.
Selectors: Methods such as getElementById, getElementsByClassName, and querySelector help you select elements.
Dynamic Manipulation: You can change content, styles, and even add or remove elements from the document.

Coding Tip
Tip: Use querySelector for flexibility with CSS selectors, and querySelectorAll when you need to work with multiple elements at once.

Code Example
```
<!DOCTYPE html>
<html lang="en">
<head>
```

```
<meta charset="UTF-8">
<title>DOM Introduction</title>
</head>
<body>
  <h1 id="title">Hello, World!</h1>
  <p class="description">This is a sample
paragraph.</p>
  <script>
    // Accessing an element by its ID
    const titleElement =
document.getElementById("title");
    console.log("Title:",
titleElement.textContent);
    // Using querySelector to access an
element by class
    const descElement =
document.querySelector(".description");
    console.log("Description:",
descElement.textContent);
  </script>
</body>
</html>
```

Section 2: Manipulating DOM Elements

Once you have selected an element, you can manipulate its
content, style, attributes, and even its structure.

Detailed Explanation
Changing Content: Use textContent or innerHTML to update
the content.

Modifying Styles: Change an element's CSS properties via the
style property.
Managing Attributes: Use methods like setAttribute,
getAttribute, and removeAttribute.

Creating and Removing Elements: Dynamically create elements with document.createElement and add them to the DOM with methods like appendChild.

Code Examples

Example 1 – Updating Text and HTML:
```
// Update the text content
titleElement.textContent = "Welcome to DOM
Manipulation!";
// Update the inner HTML
descElement.innerHTML = "<strong>This is a
bolded description.</strong>";
```

Example 2 – Changing Styles:
```
titleElement.style.color = "blue";
descElement.style.fontSize = "18px";
```

Example 3 – Creating and Appending Elements:
```
// Create a new paragraph element
let newParagraph =
document.createElement("p");
newParagraph.textContent = "This paragraph was
added dynamically.";
// Append it to the body
document.body.appendChild(newParagraph);
```

Section 3: Event Handling

Events are actions or occurrences (like clicks or key presses) that happen in the browser. JavaScript uses event listeners to run code in response to these events.

Detailed Explanation

Adding Event Listeners: Use addEventListener to attach events to elements.

Event Types: Common events include click, mouseover, keydown, and submit.

Event Object: Event listeners receive an event object containing details about the event.
Preventing Default Behavior: Use event.preventDefault() to stop default actions, such as form submissions.

Code Examples

Example 1 – Click Event:
```
// Select a button element
const button =
document.createElement("button");
button.textContent = "Click Me!";
document.body.appendChild(button);
// Add a click event listener
button.addEventListener("click",
function(event) {
  alert("Button was clicked!");
});
```

Example 2 – Form Submission:
```
<form id="contactForm">
  <input type="text" placeholder="Enter your name" id="nameInput" required>
  <button type="submit">Submit</button>
</form>
<script>
  const form =
document.getElementById("contactForm");
  form.addEventListener("submit",
function(event) {
    event.preventDefault(); // Prevent the
form from submitting
    const name =
document.getElementById("nameInput").value;
```

```
      console.log("Form submitted. Name:",
name);
  });
</script>
```

Section 4: Practical Mini Project – Interactive Web Page

Let's build a simple interactive web page that combines DOM manipulation and event handling. The page will include a list of items that the user can add to, remove from, and update dynamically.

Project Overview
Features:

Add new items to a list.

Remove items from the list.
Update item text when clicked.
Techniques: DOM selection, event listeners, creating and removing elements.

Code Example
```
<!DOCTYPE html>
<html lang="en">
<head>
  <meta charset="UTF-8">
  <title>Interactive List</title>
  <style>
    li { cursor: pointer; margin: 5px 0; }
  </style>
</head>
<body>
  <h2>My To-Do List</h2>
```

```html
  <input type="text" id="itemInput"
placeholder="Enter new item">
  <button id="addButton">Add Item</button>
  <ul id="todoList"></ul>
  <script>
    const addButton =
document.getElementById("addButton");
    const itemInput =
document.getElementById("itemInput");
    const todoList =
document.getElementById("todoList");
    // Function to add a new list item
    function addItem() {
      const itemText = itemInput.value.trim();
      if (itemText !== "") {
        const li =
document.createElement("li");
        li.textContent = itemText;
        // Add click event to update item text
        li.addEventListener("click",
function() {
          const newText = prompt("Update
item:", li.textContent);
          if (newText) {
            li.textContent = newText;
          }
        });
        // Add right-click event to remove
item
        li.addEventListener("contextmenu",
function(e) {
          e.preventDefault();
          li.remove();
        });
        todoList.appendChild(li);
        itemInput.value = "";
```

```
        }
    }
    addButton.addEventListener("click",
addItem);
    // Optionally, add an event listener for
the Enter key
    itemInput.addEventListener("keydown",
function(e) {
        if (e.key === "Enter") {
          addItem();
        }
    });
  </script>
</body>
</html>
```

Section 5: Coding Exercises

Below are 15 exercises designed to give you extra practice with DOM manipulation and event handling.

Exercise 1 – Access and Modify Content
Task: Create an HTML page with an <h1> element with id "header". Use JavaScript to change its text to "DOM is Awesome!".

Exercise 2 – Change Element Styles
Task: Create a `<div>` with class `"box"` and set its initial background color. Then, write JS to change the color to `"green"` when the page loads.
`document.querySelector(".box").style.backgroun dColor = "green";`

Exercise 3 – Create and Append Elements
Task: Dynamically create a <ul> element with three <li> items and append it to the body.

Exercise 4 – Remove an Element
Task: Create a button that, when clicked, removes a specific
<p> element from the page.

Exercise 5 – Update Attributes
Task: Create an image element with a placeholder image.
Write JS to change its src attribute to a new image URL when a
button is clicked.

Exercise 6 – Toggle Visibility
Task: Create a paragraph and a button. Write code so that
clicking the button toggles the visibility of the paragraph.

Exercise 7 – Event Listener for Multiple Elements
Task: Create three buttons. Write code to attach the same click
event listener to all buttons that logs the button text.

Exercise 8 – Input Field Listener
Task: Create an input field and log its current value to the
console every time the user types a key (use the input event).

Exercise 9 – Change Text on Hover
Task: Create a <div> with some text. Change the text color
when the mouse hovers over the div, and revert when the
mouse leaves.

Exercise 10 – Form Validation
Task: Create a simple form with an email input. Prevent
submission if the email does not contain an "@" symbol and
display an alert.

Exercise 11 – Dynamic List Update
Task: Create a list of names. Write code so that when a name is
clicked, it is removed from the list.

Exercise 12 – Counter with Buttons
Task: Create a counter displayed in a <span>, with two
buttons labeled "Increment" and "Decrement". Update the
counter value when buttons are clicked.

Exercise 13 – Delayed Content Update
Task: Use setTimeout to change the text of an element after 3 seconds.

Exercise 14 – Event Delegation
Task: Create a <ul> with several <li> items. Instead of adding click events to each <li>, add one event listener to the <ul> that logs the text of the clicked <li>.

Exercise 15 – Interactive Style Changer
Task: Create a set of buttons that, when clicked, change the background color of the page to the color indicated by the button's text.

Section 6: Multiple Choice Quiz – DOM and Events

What does DOM stand for?
A. Document Object Model
B. Data Object Method
C. Document Oriented Management
D. Dynamic Object Module
Correct Answer: A

Which method is used to select an element by its ID?
A. document.querySelector
B. document.getElementById
C. document.getElement
D. document.getElementByClass
Correct Answer: B

How do you select the first element that matches a CSS selector?
A. querySelector
B. getElementsByTagName
C. querySelectorAll
D. getElementById
Correct Answer: A

What property is used to change the text content of an element?
A. innerText
B. textContent
C. contentText
D. both A and B
Correct Answer: D

Which method creates a new HTML element?
A. document.newElement()
B. document.createElement()
C. document.appendElement()
D. document.makeElement()
Correct Answer: B

How do you add a new child element to a parent element?
A. parent.appendChild(child)
B. parent.addChild(child)
C. parent.append(child)
D. Both A and C can work
Correct Answer: D

What event is typically used to execute code when a button is clicked?
A. mouseover
B. click
C. change
D. keydown
Correct Answer: B

Which method is used to stop a form from submitting and reloading the page?
A. event.stop()
B. event.cancel()
C. event.preventDefault()
D. event.halt()
Correct Answer: C

What is the purpose of addEventListener?
A. To attach a function that runs when an event occurs
B. To remove an element from the DOM
C. To update the style of an element
D. To create a new HTML element
Correct Answer: A

Which property of an element is used to update its CSS style in JavaScript?
A. style
B. css
C. className
D. attribute
Correct Answer: A

How can you prevent the default action of an event?
A. return false;
B. event.stopPropagation();
C. event.preventDefault();
D. Both A and C
Correct Answer: D

Which event is fired when the DOM is fully loaded?
A. window.load
B. DOMContentLoaded
C. document.ready
D. pageLoaded
Correct Answer: B

What does the querySelectorAll method return?
A. A single element
B. An array of elements
C. A NodeList
D. A string
Correct Answer: C

Which event would you use to detect when the mouse pointer leaves an element?
A. mouseover
B. mouseenter
C. mouseleave
D. mouseout
Correct Answer: C

What does the remove() method do?
A. Removes an element from its parent in the DOM
B. Removes an event listener
C. Removes an attribute from an element
D. Removes the inner text of an element
Correct Answer: A

Which of the following is NOT a valid way to access a DOM element?
A. document.getElementById("id")
B. document.getElementsByClassName("class")
C. document.querySelector("selector")
D. document.find("selector")
Correct Answer: D

Event delegation is a technique used to: A. Attach an event listener to multiple elements individually
B. Attach a single event listener to a parent element to handle events on its children
C. Remove all event listeners from an element
D. Delegate events to a different document
Correct Answer: B

Which method can be used to change an element's attribute?
A. setAttribute()
B. changeAttribute()
C. updateAttribute()
D. modifyAttribute()
Correct Answer: A

What does innerHTML allow you to do?
A. Get or set the HTML markup inside an element
B. Get or set plain text inside an element
C. Add a new element to the DOM
D. Change the CSS styles of an element
Correct Answer: A

Which event property gives you details about the event, such as which key was pressed?
A. event.info
B. event.data
C. event.detail
D. The event object itself
Correct Answer: D

Recap & Next Steps

In this chapter, you learned how to:

Access and modify DOM elements using a variety of methods and selectors.

Dynamically change content and styles, create and remove elements, and update attributes.
Attach event listeners to handle user interactions such as clicks, hovers, and form submissions.

Build an interactive mini project that combines these techniques into a real-world application.

Final Coding Tip

As you build interactive pages, break your code into small, reusable functions and test each component independently. Use console logging generously to trace and debug your changes.

By working through these exercises and quizzes, you've built a solid foundation in DOM manipulation and event handling. These skills are essential for creating dynamic, responsive web applications. In the next chapter, we'll explore asynchronous programming and APIs to further expand your JavaScript toolkit.

Chapter 5: Asynchronous Programming and APIs

Modern web applications often need to perform tasks like fetching data from a server, handling time-based events, or processing large computations without blocking the user interface. In JavaScript, asynchronous programming is the key to achieving smooth, non-blocking behavior. In this chapter, you will learn to:

- Understand asynchronous programming and the JavaScript event loop.
- Work with callbacks, Promises, and async/await to handle asynchronous operations.
- Use the Fetch API to communicate with external APIs and process JSON data.

- Practice error handling in asynchronous code.

Section 1: Understanding Asynchronous Programming

JavaScript is single-threaded, meaning it executes code in a single sequence. Asynchronous programming allows you to perform long-running operations (like network requests or timers) without blocking other operations. The event loop and callback queue work together to handle asynchronous tasks.

Code Example: Synchronous vs. Asynchronous

```
// Synchronous example
console.log("Start");
for (let i = 0; i < 1000000000; i++) {} //
Time-consuming loop
console.log("End"); // This will run only
after the loop completes
// Asynchronous example using setTimeout
console.log("Start");
setTimeout(() => {
  console.log("This runs asynchronously after
2 seconds");
}, 2000);
console.log("End"); // This logs immediately
after "Start"
```

Coding Tip

Tip: Use asynchronous techniques to ensure that long-running tasks (such as API calls or heavy computations) do not freeze the user interface.

Section 2: Callbacks

A callback is a function passed as an argument to another function, which is then invoked after some operation has completed.

Code Example: Basic Callback with setTimeout

```
function greet(name, callback) {
  console.log(`Hello, ${name}!`);
  callback();
}
function sayGoodbye() {
  console.log("Goodbye!");
}
```

```
// Calling greet and passing sayGoodbye as a
callback
greet("Alice", sayGoodbye);
```

Coding Exercise 1

Exercise: Write a function `doTask` that accepts a task description (string) and a callback function. Log "`Starting: [task]`" and then, after a 1-second delay, execute the callback that logs "`Completed: [task]`".

```
function doTask(task, callback) {
  console.log(`Starting: ${task}`);
  setTimeout(() => {
    callback(task);
  }, 1000);
}
doTask("Loading Data", (task) => {
  console.log(`Completed: ${task}`);
});
```

Section 3: Promises

Promises provide a cleaner way to handle asynchronous operations by representing a value that may be available now, later, or never.

Code Example: Creating and Using a Promise
```
function fetchData() {
  return new Promise((resolve, reject) => {
    // Simulate an asynchronous operation
using setTimeout
    setTimeout(() => {
      const success = true; // Change to false
to simulate an error
      if (success) {
        resolve({ data: "Sample Data" });
```

```
    } else {
        reject("Error fetching data");
    }
  }, 1500);
});
}
fetchData()
  .then(response => {
    console.log("Data received:",
response.data);
  })
  .catch(error => {
    console.error("Error:", error);
  });
```

Coding Exercise 2
Exercise: Create a function `simulateLogin` that returns a Promise. After 1.5 seconds, resolve the promise with a message `"Login successful"` if a provided username equals `"user"`; otherwise, reject it with `"Invalid username"`.

```
function simulateLogin(username) {
  return new Promise((resolve, reject) => {
    setTimeout(() => {
      if (username === "user") {
        resolve("Login successful");
      } else {
        reject("Invalid username");
      }
    }, 1500);
  });
}
simulateLogin("user")
  .then(msg => console.log(msg))
  .catch(err => console.error(err));
```

Section 4: Async/Await

Async/await is a syntactic sugar built on top of Promises that makes asynchronous code look and behave more like synchronous code.

Code Example: Converting Promises to Async/Await

```
async function getData() {
  try {
    const response = await fetchData(); //
fetchData from the previous example
    console.log("Async/Await Data:",
response.data);
  } catch (error) {
    console.error("Error in async/await:",
error);
  }
}
getData();
```

Coding Exercise 3

Exercise: Rewrite the `simulateLogin` function call using async/await. Create an async function `loginUser` that awaits `simulateLogin` and logs the result.

```
async function loginUser(username) {
  try {
    const message = await
simulateLogin(username);
    console.log(message);
  } catch (error) {
    console.error(error);
  }
}
loginUser("wrongUser"); // Should log error
message
```

```
loginUser("user");      // Should log "Login
successful"
```

Section 5: Working with the Fetch API

The Fetch API allows you to make network requests to retrieve or send data. It returns a Promise that resolves to the Response object representing the response to your request.

Code Example: Basic Fetch Request
```
async function fetchPosts() {
  try {
    const response = await
fetch("https://jsonplaceholder.typicode.com/po
sts");
    // Check if the response is ok (status in
the range 200-299)
    if (!response.ok) {
      throw new Error("Network response was
not ok");
    }
    const posts = await response.json();
    console.log("Fetched Posts:",
posts.slice(0, 3)); // Log first 3 posts for
brevity
  } catch (error) {
    console.error("Fetch error:", error);
  }
}
fetchPosts();
```

Coding Exercise 4

Exercise: Create a function `fetchUserData` that uses fetch to retrieve data from "`https://jsonplaceholder.typicode.com/users`". Log the names of the users.

```
async function fetchUserData() {
  try {
    const response = await
fetch("https://jsonplaceholder.typicode.com/us
ers");
    if (!response.ok) throw new Error("Failed
to fetch user data");
    const users = await response.json();
    users.forEach(user =>
console.log(user.name));
  } catch (error) {
    console.error("Error fetching user data:",
error);
  }
}
fetchUserData();
```

Section 6: Additional Coding Exercises

Here are several more exercises to help you practice asynchronous programming and working with APIs:

Exercise 5 – Delayed Greeting

Task: Create a function `delayedGreeting` that returns a Promise. After 2 seconds, it should resolve with "`Hello after 2 seconds!`" and log the message using async/await.

```
function delayedGreeting() {
  return new Promise(resolve => {
    setTimeout(() => {
      resolve("Hello after 2 seconds!");
```

```
    }, 2000);
  });
}
async function greet() {
  const message = await delayedGreeting();
  console.log(message);
}
greet();
```

Exercise 6 – Multiple Promises

Task: Write two functions that return Promises, one that resolves after 1 second and another after 2 seconds. Use `Promise.all` to log both results together.

```
function firstTask() {
  return new Promise(resolve => {
    setTimeout(() => resolve("First task
complete"), 1000);
  });
}
function secondTask() {
  return new Promise(resolve => {
    setTimeout(() => resolve("Second task
complete"), 2000);
  });
}
Promise.all([firstTask(), secondTask()])
  .then(results => console.log("Results:",
results))
  .catch(error => console.error(error));
```

Exercise 7 – Race Condition

Task: Use `Promise.race` with two promises (one resolves in 1.5 seconds and one in 3 seconds) to log the result of the first completed promise.

```
function taskA() {
  return new Promise(resolve => {
```

```
    setTimeout(() => resolve("Task A
finished"), 1500);
  });
}
function taskB() {
  return new Promise(resolve => {
    setTimeout(() => resolve("Task B
finished"), 3000);
  });
}
Promise.race([taskA(), taskB()])
  .then(result => console.log("First
finished:", result))
  .catch(error => console.error(error));
```

Exercise 8 – Fetch and Display Data

Task: Create a small web page that fetches data from
`"https://jsonplaceholder.typicode.com/todos/1"`
and displays the todo title in an HTML element.

```
<!DOCTYPE html>
<html lang="en">
<head>
  <meta charset="UTF-8">
  <title>Todo Display</title>
</head>
<body>
  <h2 id="todoTitle">Loading...</h2>
  <script>
    async function displayTodo() {
      try {
        const res = await
fetch("https://jsonplaceholder.typicode.com/to
dos/1");
        if (!res.ok) throw new Error("Failed
to load todo");
        const todo = await res.json();
```

```
document.getElementById("todoTitle").textConte
nt = todo.title;
        } catch (error) {

document.getElementById("todoTitle").textConte
nt = "Error loading todo";
          console.error(error);
        }
      }
      displayTodo();
    </script>
</body>
</html>
```

Exercise 9 – Error Handling Practice

Task: Modify one of your previous fetch functions to intentionally request a non-existent URL. Use try/catch to handle the error gracefully and log "Request failed" if an error occurs.

```
async function fetchInvalid() {
  try {
    const res = await
fetch("https://jsonplaceholder.typicode.com/in
validurl");
    if (!res.ok) throw new Error("Network
response not ok");
    const data = await res.json();
    console.log(data);
  } catch (error) {
    console.error("Request failed:", error);
  }
}
fetchInvalid();
```

Exercise 10 – Sequential Async Calls

Task: Create an async function that awaits three different asynchronous operations in sequence (e.g., delayedGreeting, firstTask, and secondTask). Log each result as it is returned.

```
async function sequentialOperations() {
  const greeting = await delayedGreeting();
  console.log(greeting);
  const resultA = await firstTask();
  console.log(resultA);
  const resultB = await secondTask();
  console.log(resultB);
}
sequentialOperations();
```

Section 7: Multiple Choice Quiz – Asynchronous Programming & APIs

What does the term "asynchronous" mean in JavaScript?
A. Code that runs in a separate thread
B. Code that does not block execution while waiting for an operation to complete
C. Code that runs sequentially
D. Code that runs only after the DOM is loaded
Correct Answer: B

Which function is commonly used to simulate a delay in asynchronous code?
A. setInterval()
B. setTimeout()
C. delay()
D. asyncDelay()
Correct Answer: B

What does a Promise represent in JavaScript?
A. A value that is always available immediately
B. A value that may be available now, later, or never
C. A function that always returns data
D. An error handler
Correct Answer: B

How do you handle errors in a Promise chain?
A. Using .catch()
B. Using try/catch
C. Using .then() only
D. Errors cannot be handled in Promises
Correct Answer: A

Which syntax allows you to write asynchronous code that looks synchronous?
A. .then()
B. async/await
C. Callbacks
D. Promises
Correct Answer: B

What is the purpose of the async keyword before a function declaration?
A. It makes the function execute synchronously
B. It enables the use of await inside the function
C. It automatically catches errors
D. It converts the function to a Promise
Correct Answer: B
(Note: Declaring a function as async also makes it return a Promise.)

Which method is used to make network requests in modern JavaScript?
A. XMLHttpRequest
B. jQuery.ajax()
C. Fetch API
D. sendRequest()
Correct Answer: C

What does the fetch() function return?

A. An array

B. A Promise that resolves to a Response object

C. A JSON object

D. A string

Correct Answer: B

How do you convert a Response object to JSON?

A. response.toJSON()

B. JSON.parse(response)

C. response.json()

D. response.convert()

Correct Answer: C

What is the use of Promise.all()?

A. To execute Promises sequentially

B. To execute multiple Promises in parallel and wait for all to resolve

C. To catch errors in Promises

D. To convert callbacks to Promises

Correct Answer: B

Which operator is used with async/await to wait for a Promise to resolve?

A. yield

B. await

C. then

D. async

Correct Answer: B

How can you run multiple asynchronous operations concurrently and use the first one to finish?

A. Promise.all()

B. Promise.race()

C. async/await

D. Callback hell

Correct Answer: B

What will the following code log?

```
setTimeout(() => console.log("Delayed"), 0);
console.log("Immediate");
```

A. "Delayed" then "Immediate"
B. "Immediate" then "Delayed"
C. Only "Immediate"
D. Only "Delayed"
Correct Answer: B
In async/await, how do you handle errors?
A. Using .then()
B. Using .catch() chained to await
C. Using try/catch blocks
D. Errors are ignored
Correct Answer: C
Which of the following best describes a callback?
A. A synchronous function call
B. A function passed as an argument to another function
C. A Promise resolution method
D. A method to cancel asynchronous operations
Correct Answer: B
What will the following code snippet output?

```
async function test() {
   return "Hello";
}
console.log(test());
```

A. "Hello"
B. Promise { "Hello" }
C. undefined
D. Error
Correct Answer: B
Which statement is true about async functions?
A. They always block the main thread
B. They always return a Promise
C. They cannot handle errors
D. They are executed before synchronous code
Correct Answer: B

What is the benefit of using async/await over traditional Promises?
A. It makes code shorter and more readable
B. It prevents all errors
C. It eliminates the need for the event loop
D. It makes synchronous code run faster
Correct Answer: A

How can you simulate a delay using Promises?
A. Using setTimeout inside a Promise constructor
B. Using Promise.delay()
C. Using asyncDelay()
D. It is not possible
Correct Answer: A
Which of the following is NOT a method of handling asynchronous operations in JavaScript?
A. Callbacks
B. Promises
C. async/await
D. Synchronous loops
Correct Answer: D

Recap & Next Steps

In this chapter, you learned to:

Understand asynchronous programming and why it's essential for responsive web applications.
Use callbacks, Promises, and async/await to manage asynchronous tasks in different scenarios.
Make network requests with the Fetch API and handle JSON responses.
Practice error handling in asynchronous code to build robust applications.

Final Coding Tip

When dealing with asynchronous operations, break your tasks into small, testable functions. Use async/await for cleaner, easier-to-read code, and always handle errors gracefully with try/catch blocks.

By working through the detailed examples, coding exercises, and quizzes in this chapter, you've built a strong foundation in asynchronous programming and API integration. These skills are crucial as you develop more interactive and dynamic web applications. In the next chapter, we'll explore advanced topics like working with third-party libraries, optimizing performance, and further enhancing your web development toolkit.

Chapter 6: Advanced JavaScript – Closures, Prototypes, and Classes

Modern JavaScript isn't just about writing functions and handling events — it also includes advanced concepts that empower you to write encapsulated, reusable code. In this chapter, we cover:
- Closures and Lexical Scope
- The this Keyword and Execution Context
- Prototype Inheritance
- Classes in JavaScript
- Mini Project: Object-Oriented Task Manager
- Additional Coding Exercises

- Multiple Choice Quiz

Section 1: Closures and Lexical Scope

Closures allow a function to remember the environment (variables, parameters) in which it was created — even after that outer function has finished executing. This leads to powerful patterns like data encapsulation and function factories.

Detailed Explanation

Lexical Scope: Variables defined outside a function are accessible within that function.
Closure: A function "closes over" the variables from its surrounding scope. This means it retains access to them even when executed outside their original scope.

Code Examples

Example 1 – Basic Closure:
```
function makeCounter() {
  let count = 0; // private variable
  return function() {
    count++;
    return count;
  };
}
const counter = makeCounter();
console.log(counter()); // Output: 1
console.log(counter()); // Output: 2
```

Example 2 – Function Factory:
```
function createGreeter(greeting) {
  return function(name) {
    console.log(`${greeting}, ${name}!`);
  };
}
const sayHello = createGreeter("Hello");
sayHello("Alice"); // Output: Hello, Alice!
```

Coding Exercises
Exercise 1 – Private Variable with Closure
Task: Write a function `createSecretHolder` that accepts a secret and returns an object with two methods: `getSecret` (to return the secret) and `setSecret` (to change it).

```
function createSecretHolder(secret) {
  return {
    getSecret() {
      return secret;
    },
    setSecret(newSecret) {
      secret = newSecret;
    }
  };
}
const secretHolder =
createSecretHolder("mySecret");
console.log(secretHolder.getSecret()); //
Output: mySecret
secretHolder.setSecret("newSecret");
console.log(secretHolder.getSecret()); //
Output: newSecret
```

Exercise 2 – Counter with Increment and Decrement
Task: Create a function `createCounter` that returns an object with `increment` and `decrement` methods, using a private counter variable.

```
function createCounter() {
  let count = 0;
  return {
    increment() {
      count++;
      return count;
    },
    decrement() {
```

```
      count--;
      return count;
    }
  };
}
const counterObj = createCounter();
console.log(counterObj.increment()); // 1
console.log(counterObj.decrement()); // 0
```

Exercise 3 – Closure with Array State

Task: Write a function `createListManager` that maintains a private array. Include methods to add an item, remove an item by value, and list all items.

```
function createListManager() {
  const list = [];
  return {
    add(item) {
      list.push(item);
    },
    remove(item) {
      const index = list.indexOf(item);
      if (index > -1) list.splice(index, 1);
    },
    getList() {
      return [...list];
    }
  };
}
const listManager = createListManager();
listManager.add("apple");
listManager.add("banana");
console.log(listManager.getList()); //
["apple", "banana"]
listManager.remove("apple");
console.log(listManager.getList()); //
["banana"]
```

Section 2: The this Keyword and Execution Context

Understanding **this** is crucial for writing object-oriented code in JavaScript. The value of **this** depends on how a function is called rather than where it is defined.

Detailed Explanation

Global Context: In non-strict mode, this in the global context refers to the global object (window in browsers). In strict mode, it is undefined.

Object Method: When a function is called as a method of an object, this refers to that object.

Arrow Functions: They do not have their own this; they inherit it from the parent scope.

Explicit Binding: Methods like call(), apply(), and bind() allow you to set this explicitly.

Code Examples

Example 1 – Object Method:

```
const person = {
   name: "Alice",
   greet() {
      console.log(`Hello, my name is
${this.name}`);
   }
};
person.greet(); // Output: Hello, my name is
Alice
```

Example 2 – Arrow Function and this:

```
const obj = {
   value: 42,
   show: () => {
```

```
    console.log(this.value); // 'this' here
refers to the global scope (or undefined in
strict mode)
  }
};
obj.show(); // Likely outputs undefined (or
global value)
```

Coding Exercises
Exercise 4 – Fixing this in Arrow Functions
Task: Rewrite the previous example using a regular function
so that **this** correctly refers to the object.

```
const objFixed = {
  value: 42,
  show() {
    console.log(this.value);
  }
};
objFixed.show(); // Output: 42
```

Exercise 5 – Using call() to Set this
Task: Create a function introduce that logs "My name is
[name]" using **this.name**. Then, call it with a custom object
using call().

```
function introduce() {
  console.log(`My name is ${this.name}`);
}
const user = { name: "Bob" };
introduce.call(user); // Output: My name is
Bob
```

Exercise 6 – Binding this

Task: Write a function that returns another function (using closure) which uses **this** from its enclosing context. Use bind() to ensure that **this** remains correct when the inner function is called.

```
const counterObject = {
  count: 0,
  increment() {
    this.count++;
    console.log(this.count);
  }
};
const unboundIncrement =
counterObject.increment;
// Using bind to ensure 'this' remains
counterObject
const boundIncrement =
unboundIncrement.bind(counterObject);
boundIncrement(); // Output: 1
boundIncrement(); // Output: 2
```

Section 3: Prototype Inheritance

JavaScript uses prototype-based inheritance. Every object in JavaScript has a prototype from which it can inherit properties and methods.

Detailed Explanation

Constructor Functions: Traditional way to create objects that share methods via their prototype.
Prototype Property: Functions have a prototype property where you can define methods that all instances will share.
Inheritance: You can create an inheritance chain using constructor functions or Object.create().

Code Examples

Example 1 – Constructor Function with Prototype Method:
```
function Animal(name) {
   this.name = name;
}
Animal.prototype.speak = function() {
   console.log(`${this.name} makes a sound.`);
};
const dog = new Animal("Rex");
dog.speak(); // Output: Rex makes a sound.
```

Example 2 – Using Object.create():
```
const animalProto = {
   speak() {
      console.log(`${this.name} speaks.`);
   }
};
const cat = Object.create(animalProto);
cat.name = "Whiskers";
cat.speak(); // Output: Whiskers speaks.
```

Coding Exercises
Exercise 7 – Create a Prototype Chain
Task: Create a constructor function `Vehicle` with a method
`start()`. Then, create a constructor function `Car` that inherits
from `Vehicle` and adds a method `drive()`.

```
function Vehicle(make) {
   this.make = make;
}
Vehicle.prototype.start = function() {
   console.log(`${this.make} vehicle
starting.`);
};
function Car(make, model) {
   Vehicle.call(this, make);
```

```
    this.model = model;
}
Car.prototype =
Object.create(Vehicle.prototype);
Car.prototype.constructor = Car;
Car.prototype.drive = function() {
    console.log(`${this.make} ${this.model} is
driving.`);
};
const myCar = new Car("Toyota", "Corolla");
myCar.start(); // Output: Toyota vehicle
starting.
myCar.drive(); // Output: Toyota Corolla is
driving.
```

Exercise 8 – Overriding Prototype Methods

Task: Create a constructor `Bird` with a method `fly()`. Then create a constructor `Penguin` that inherits from `Bird` but overrides `fly()` to log that penguins cannot fly.

```
function Bird(name) {
    this.name = name;
}
Bird.prototype.fly = function() {
    console.log(`${this.name} is flying.`);
};
function Penguin(name) {
    Bird.call(this, name);
}
Penguin.prototype =
Object.create(Bird.prototype);
Penguin.prototype.constructor = Penguin;
Penguin.prototype.fly = function() {
    console.log(`${this.name} cannot fly.`);
};
const penguin = new Penguin("Pingu");
penguin.fly(); // Output: Pingu cannot fly.
```

Section 4: Classes in JavaScript

ES6 introduced classes as a more familiar and concise way to create objects and handle inheritance. Under the hood, classes still use prototypes.

Detailed Explanation

Class Syntax: Provides a clear, declarative way to define constructors and methods.

Constructor Method: Special method for initializing new objects.
Inheritance: Use the extends keyword to create subclasses, and super() to call the parent constructor.

Code Examples

Example 1 – Basic Class:

```
class Person {
  constructor(name, age) {
    this.name = name;
    this.age = age;
  }
  greet() {
    console.log(`Hello, I'm ${this.name} and
I'm ${this.age} years old.`);
  }
}
const alice = new Person("Alice", 28);
alice.greet(); // Output: Hello, I'm Alice and
I'm 28 years old.
```

Example 2 – Class Inheritance:

```
class Student extends Person {
  constructor(name, age, grade) {
    super(name, age);
```

```
    this.grade = grade;
  }
  study() {
    console.log(`${this.name} is studying for
grade ${this.grade}.`);
  }
}
const bob = new Student("Bob", 20, "A");
bob.greet();  // Inherited method
bob.study();  // Output: Bob is studying for
grade A.
```

Coding Exercises
Exercise 9 – Create a Basic Class
Task: Write a class Animal with a constructor that takes a name and a method speak() that logs "name makes a sound".

```
class Animal {
  constructor(name) {
    this.name = name;
  }
  speak() {
    console.log(`${this.name} makes a
sound.`);
  }
}
const animal = new Animal("Generic Animal");
animal.speak();
```
Exercise 10 – Extend a Class
Task: Create a class Dog that extends Animal and overrides speak() to log "name barks".

```
class Dog extends Animal {
  speak() {
    console.log(`${this.name} barks.`);
```

```
  }
}
const dog = new Dog("Rex");
dog.speak(); // Output: Rex barks.
```
Exercise 11 – Static Methods

Task: Add a static method `info()` to the `Person` class that logs `"This is the Person class."`.

```
class Person {
  constructor(name, age) {
    this.name = name;
    this.age = age;
  }
  greet() {
    console.log(`Hello, I'm ${this.name} and
I'm ${this.age} years old.`);
  }
  static info() {
    console.log("This is the Person class.");
  }
}
Person.info(); // Output: This is the Person
class.
```

Section 5: Mini Project – Object-Oriented Task Manager

In this mini project, you'll build a simple Task Manager using classes and closures to encapsulate functionality.

Project Overview

Task Class: Represents a single task with properties like title, description, and status. Include methods to mark the task as complete.

TaskManager Class: Manages a list of tasks. Include methods to add, remove, and list tasks.
Encapsulation: Use private variables via closures if desired for extra practice.

Code Example

```
class Task {
  constructor(title, description) {
    this.title = title;
    this.description = description;
    this.completed = false;
  }
  markComplete() {
    this.completed = true;
    console.log(`Task "${this.title}" marked
as complete.`);
  }
  display() {
    console.log(`Title: ${this.title}`);
    console.log(`Description:
${this.description}`);
    console.log(`Status: ${this.completed ?
"Completed" : "Incomplete"}`);
  }
}
class TaskManager {
  constructor() {
    this.tasks = [];
  }
  addTask(task) {
    this.tasks.push(task);
    console.log(`Task "${task.title}"
added.`);
  }
  removeTask(title) {
```

```
    this.tasks = this.tasks.filter(task =>
task.title !== title);
    console.log(`Task "${title}" removed.`);
  }
  listTasks() {
    console.log("Listing Tasks:");
    this.tasks.forEach(task =>
task.display());
  }
}
// Using the Task Manager
const manager = new TaskManager();
const task1 = new Task("Buy Groceries", "Milk,
Bread, Eggs");
const task2 = new Task("Clean Room", "Organize
books and clean the floor");
manager.addTask(task1);
manager.addTask(task2);
manager.listTasks();
task1.markComplete();
manager.listTasks();
manager.removeTask("Clean Room");
manager.listTasks();
```

Coding Exercise
Exercise 12 – Enhance the Task Manager
Task: Add a method updateTask(title,
newDescription) to update a task's description and test it
by updating one of your tasks.

```
TaskManager.prototype.updateTask =
function(title, newDescription) {
  const task = this.tasks.find(task =>
task.title === title);
  if (task) {
    task.description = newDescription;
```

```
    console.log(`Task "${title}" updated.`);
  } else {
    console.log(`Task "${title}" not found.`);
  }
};
// Testing the update method:
manager.updateTask("Buy Groceries", "Milk,
Bread, Eggs, and Cheese");
manager.listTasks();
```

Section 6: Additional Coding Exercises

Here are several more exercises to deepen your understanding of advanced JavaScript concepts:

Exercise 13 – Create a Closure-Based Logger

Task: Write a function createLogger(prefix) that returns a logging function which prepends the prefix to all log messages.

```
function createLogger(prefix) {
  return function(message) {
    console.log(`${prefix}: ${message}`);
  };
}
const debugLogger = createLogger("DEBUG");
debugLogger("This is a debug message."); //
Output: DEBUG: This is a debug message.
```

Exercise 14 – Exploring 'this' in Nested Functions

Task: Inside an object, write a method that calls an inner regular function and an inner arrow function. Compare the output of **this** in both cases.

```
const tester = {
  value: "tester",
  testThis() {
    function regularFunction() {
```

```
      console.log("Regular function:",
this.value);
    }
    const arrowFunction = () => {
      console.log("Arrow function:",
this.value);
    };
    regularFunction();        // Likely
undefined in strict mode or global value
    arrowFunction();          // Inherits
'this' from testThis(), outputs "tester"
  }
};
tester.testThis();
```

Exercise 15 – Static vs. Instance Methods

Task: In a class, add both an instance method and a static method that return a string. Call both methods and observe the difference.

```
class Demo {
  instanceMethod() {
    return "I am an instance method";
  }
  static staticMethod() {
    return "I am a static method";
  }
}
const demoObj = new Demo();
console.log(demoObj.instanceMethod());  //
Output: I am an instance method
console.log(Demo.staticMethod());       //
Output: I am a static method
```

Section 7: Multiple Choice Quiz

What is a closure in JavaScript?
A. A function that returns another function
B. A function that remembers its lexical scope
C. A function that can access variables outside its immediate scope
D. All of the above
Correct Answer: D

Which statement best describes lexical scope?
A. Variables are accessible only in the block they are defined
B. Variables defined in an outer scope are accessible in inner functions
C. All variables are globally scoped
D. Variables are accessible only after they are declared
Correct Answer: B

In a method, what does the keyword this refer to by default?
A. The global object
B. The object that owns the method
C. The function itself
D. Undefined
Correct Answer: B

How do arrow functions differ from regular functions regarding this?
A. Arrow functions have their own this
B. Arrow functions inherit this from the parent scope
C. Arrow functions cannot access this at all
D. There is no difference
Correct Answer: B

Which method is used to explicitly set this for a function?
A. call()
B. bind()
C. apply()
D. All of the above
Correct Answer: D

What does the prototype property of a constructor function contain?
A. Instance properties
B. Methods shared among all instances
C. Private variables
D. The constructor's return value
Correct Answer: B

What is the purpose of the constructor method in a class?
A. To define static methods
B. To initialize object properties when an instance is created
C. To override prototype methods
D. To create private methods
Correct Answer: B

Which keyword is used in class inheritance to call the parent class's constructor?
A. this
B. super
C. parent
D. base
Correct Answer: B

How can you create a private variable in JavaScript using closures?
A. Declare the variable inside the outer function and return an inner function that accesses it
B. Use the private keyword
C. Declare the variable with let in the global scope
D. Use Object.defineProperty()
Correct Answer: A

Which of the following is true about static methods in classes?
A. They can be called on class instances
B. They are called on the class itself
C. They inherit from the prototype
D. They are not allowed in ES6 classes
Correct Answer: B

What is the output of this closure example?

```
function counter() {
   let count = 0;
   return function() {
      return ++count;
   };
}
const c = counter();
console.log(c()); // ?
console.log(c()); // ?
```

A. 0, 1
B. 1, 2
C. Undefined, Undefined
D. 1, 1
Correct Answer: B

Which of the following correctly creates a class in JavaScript?
A. class Person { constructor(name) { this.name = name; } }
B. function Person(name) { this.name = name; }
C. const Person = { name: "Alice" }
D. Both A and B
Correct Answer: A

What will the following code log?

```
const obj = {
   value: 100,
   show: function() {
      const inner = () =>
console.log(this.value);
      inner();
   }
};
obj.show();
```

A. Undefined
B. 100
C. Error
D. 0
Correct Answer: B

How do you override a method in a subclass?
A. Define a method with the same name in the subclass
B. Use the override keyword
C. Call super.method()
D. It is not possible
Correct Answer: A

What is the benefit of using closures for data encapsulation?
A. They allow for creating truly private variables
B. They prevent memory leaks
C. They increase execution speed
D. They simplify debugging
Correct Answer: A

Which of the following will create a new object that inherits from a given prototype?
A. new Object()
B. Object.create(proto)
C. {}
D. Object.assign()
Correct Answer: B

What does the bind() method return?
A. The original function
B. A new function with the specified this value
C. An object with methods
D. A Promise
Correct Answer: B

In a closure, if an inner function accesses a variable defined in an outer function, what is that variable called?
A. A global variable
B. A static variable
C. A free variable
D. A parameter
Correct Answer: C

Which of the following best describes prototype inheritance?
A. Inheriting properties from a class
B. Inheriting properties from another object via its prototype
C. Using closures to share data
D. None of the above
Correct Answer: B

What is the main difference between a regular function and an arrow function regarding this?
A. Arrow functions cannot have parameters
B. Regular functions do not have a this binding
C. Arrow functions inherit this from the surrounding scope
D. Regular functions always return a Promise
Correct Answer: C

Recap & Next Steps

In this chapter, you explored advanced JavaScript topics including closures, the nuances of the **this** keyword, prototype inheritance, and the modern class syntax. These concepts are essential for writing modular and maintainable code in larger applications. By working through the detailed examples and exercises, you should now feel more comfortable with these advanced patterns.

Final Coding Tip

When working with advanced JavaScript concepts, always break down your code into small, testable parts. Experiment with different patterns, use console logging to understand execution context, and leverage modern syntax (like ES6 classes) for clearer code organization.

Continue practicing these exercises and exploring more advanced topics. In upcoming chapters, you might delve into design patterns, performance optimization, or even testing frameworks to further enhance your JavaScript skills.

Chapter 7: Debugging, Testing, and Best Practices

Writing code is only part of the development process. To build robust applications, you must learn how to detect and fix errors, validate your code through testing, and follow industry best practices. In this chapter, we cover:

- Debugging Techniques: How to use browser tools, logging, and breakpoints to find issues.
- Error Handling & Logging: Best practices for handling runtime errors and logging helpful information.
- Unit Testing: How to write and run simple tests in vanilla JavaScript.
- Linting and Code Style: Tools and practices to keep your code consistent and error-free.
- Performance Optimization: Techniques like debouncing and throttling to improve responsiveness.

- Each section is packed with code examples and exercises to help you practice and master these concepts.

Section 1: Debugging Techniques

Debugging is the process of identifying and fixing bugs in your code. Modern browsers come with robust developer tools that let you inspect elements, view the call stack, set breakpoints, and more.

Detailed Explanation

Console Logging: Use console.log(), console.warn(), and console.error() to output useful information.

Breakpoints: Set breakpoints in your browser's developer tools to pause execution and inspect variables.

Step-by-Step Execution: Walk through your code line by line to determine where issues arise.

Code Examples

Example 1 – Console Logging:

```
function calculateSum(a, b) {
  console.log("calculateSum called with:", a,
b);
  const sum = a + b;
  console.log("Resulting sum:", sum);
  return sum;
}
calculateSum(5, 7);
```

Example 2 – Using Debugger Statement:

```
function processData(data) {
  // Pause execution here
  debugger;
  // Inspect variables in the dev tools
  return data.map(item => item * 2);
}
processData([1, 2, 3]);
```

Coding Exercises

Exercise 1 – Identify the Bug

Task: Write a function that multiplies two numbers but intentionally includes a mistake (e.g., using addition instead of multiplication). Use `console.log` to trace the error and fix it.

```
// Intentional error: addition instead of
multiplication
function multiply(a, b) {
  console.log("Multiplying:", a, b);
  const result = a + b; // Incorrect operation
  console.log("Result:", result);
  return result;
}
// Fix: Change '+' to '*'
function fixedMultiply(a, b) {
  console.log("Multiplying:", a, b);
  const result = a * b;
  console.log("Result:", result);
  return result;
}
multiply(3, 4);        // Debug and observe the
incorrect result
fixedMultiply(3, 4); // Should output 12
```

Exercise 2 – Using Breakpoints

Task: Create a simple loop that logs numbers 1 through 5. Set a breakpoint inside the loop (using the `debugger` statement) and inspect the loop variable.

```
for (let i = 1; i <= 5; i++) {
  debugger; // Pause here to inspect 'i'
  console.log("Number:", i);
}
```

Section 2: Error Handling & Logging

Effective error handling ensures that your application can gracefully manage unexpected situations. Use try/catch blocks and meaningful logging to diagnose issues.

Detailed Explanation

Try/Catch: Wrap code that might throw errors to prevent your application from crashing.

Custom Error Messages: Create informative error messages that help pinpoint issues.

Logging Errors: Use console.error() to log error details.

Code Examples

Example 1 – Try/Catch:

```
function parseJSON(jsonString) {
  try {
    const data = JSON.parse(jsonString);
    return data;
  } catch (error) {
    console.error("Failed to parse JSON:",
error);
    return null;
  }
}
parseJSON('{"name": "Alice"}');   // Valid
JSON
parseJSON("invalid json");        // Triggers
error handling
```

Example 2 – Custom Error Handling:

```
function divide(a, b) {
  if (b === 0) {
    throw new Error("Division by zero is not
allowed.");
  }
```

```
  return a / b;
}
try {
  console.log(divide(10, 0));
} catch (error) {
  console.error("Error during division:",
error.message);
}
```

Coding Exercises
Exercise 3 – Handle JSON Parse Errors
Task: Create a function that safely parses a JSON string. If parsing fails, log "Parsing error occurred" and return an empty object.

```
function safeParse(jsonString) {
  try {
    return JSON.parse(jsonString);
  } catch (error) {
    console.error("Parsing error occurred:",
error.message);
    return {};
  }
}
console.log(safeParse('{"valid": true}'));
console.log(safeParse("invalid json"));
```

Exercise 4 – Custom Error Throwing
Task: Write a function checkAge(age) that throws an error if age is less than 18. Catch and log the error.

```
function checkAge(age) {
  if (age < 18) {
    throw new Error("Age must be at least
18.");
  }
  return "Access granted";
}
try {
```

```
  console.log(checkAge(16));
} catch (error) {
  console.error("Error:", error.message);
}
```

Section 3: Unit Testing in Vanilla JavaScript

Testing your code ensures that each part works as expected. While many frameworks exist (like Mocha or Jest), you can write simple tests using assertions in vanilla JavaScript.

Detailed Explanation

Assertions: Check if a value matches the expected result.

Test Functions: Create small functions that run tests and log results.
Automated Testing: Write tests for functions to catch errors before deployment.

Code Examples

Example 1 – Simple Assertion Function:
```
function assertEqual(actual, expected,
testName) {
  if (actual === expected) {
    console.log(`PASSED [${testName}]`);
  } else {
    console.error(`FAILED [${testName}]:
Expected "${expected}", but got "${actual}"`);
  }
}
// Example test
function add(a, b) {
  return a + b;
}
```

```
assertEqual(add(2, 3), 5, "add() should return
the sum of two numbers");
assertEqual(add(2, 3), 6, "add() should return
the sum of two numbers (intentional
failure)");
```

Example 2 – Testing Asynchronous Code:
```
function asyncAdd(a, b, callback) {
  setTimeout(() => {
    callback(a + b);
  }, 500);
}
function testAsyncAdd() {
  asyncAdd(4, 5, (result) => {
    assertEqual(result, 9, "asyncAdd() should
return the sum after a delay");
  });
}
testAsyncAdd();
```

Coding Exercises
Exercise 5 – Write Unit Tests for Subtraction
Task: Write a function subtract(a, b) and create at least
two tests using an assertion function.
```
function subtract(a, b) {
  return a - b;
}
// Tests
assertEqual(subtract(10, 5), 5, "subtract()
should return the difference");
assertEqual(subtract(5, 10), -5, "subtract()
should handle negative results");
```

Exercise 6 – Create an Async Test

Task: Write a function `asyncMultiply(a, b, callback)` that multiplies two numbers after 300ms, then write a test for it.

```
function asyncMultiply(a, b, callback) {
  setTimeout(() => {
    callback(a * b);
  }, 300);
}
asyncMultiply(3, 4, (result) => {
  assertEqual(result, 12, "asyncMultiply()
should return the product of two numbers");
});
```

Section 4: Linting and Code Style

Consistent code style and linting help you avoid common mistakes and improve readability. Tools like ESLint can automatically check your code for errors and enforce style guidelines.

Detailed Explanation

ESLint: A popular tool that analyzes your JavaScript code for potential errors.
Code Style: Consistent indentation, naming conventions, and commenting practices make code easier to understand.
Configuration Files: Use a configuration file (like .eslintrc.json) to define rules for your project.

Code Example

Example – A Simple ESLint Configuration (JSON):

```
{
  "env": {
    "browser": true,
    "es6": true
  },
```

```
"extends": "eslint:recommended",
"rules": {
  "indent": ["error", 2],
  "quotes": ["error", "single"],
  "semi": ["error", "always"]
}
}
```

Coding Exercises
Exercise 7 – Refactor Code to Meet Linting Rules
Task: Take a block of poorly formatted code, reformat it according to common ESLint rules, and add comments explaining your changes.

```
// Before refactoring:
function badStyle(){console.log("bad style");}
// After refactoring:
function goodStyle() {
  console.log('good style');
}
goodStyle();
```

Section 5: Performance Optimization Techniques

Optimizing your code can improve the user experience by making your application more responsive. Two common techniques are debouncing and throttling.

Detailed Explanation

Debouncing: Ensures that a function is only called after a certain period of inactivity.

Throttling: Ensures that a function is called at most once in a specified period.
Use Cases: Useful in scenarios like window resizing, scrolling, or keypress events.

Code Examples

Example 1 – Debouncing Function:

```javascript
function debounce(func, delay) {
  let timeoutId;
  return function (...args) {
    clearTimeout(timeoutId);
    timeoutId = setTimeout(() => {
      func.apply(this, args);
    }, delay);
  };
}
// Usage:
const handleResize = debounce(() => {
  console.log('Window resized!');
}, 500);
window.addEventListener('resize',
handleResize);
```

Example 2 – Throttling Function:

```javascript
function throttle(func, limit) {
  let inThrottle;
  return function (...args) {
    if (!inThrottle) {
      func.apply(this, args);
      inThrottle = true;
      setTimeout(() => inThrottle = false,
limit);
    }
  };
}
// Usage:
const handleScroll = throttle(() => {
  console.log('Scroll event handled!');
}, 1000);
```

```
window.addEventListener('scroll',
handleScroll);
```

Coding Exercises
Exercise 8 – Implement Debounce
Task: Write your own version of a debounce function and use it to log keystrokes from an input field only after the user stops typing for 400ms.

```
<input type="text" id="debounceInput"
placeholder="Type something...">
<script>
  function debounce(func, delay) {
    let timeoutId;
    return function (...args) {
      clearTimeout(timeoutId);
      timeoutId = setTimeout(() =>
func.apply(this, args), delay);
    };
  }
  const inputField =
document.getElementById("debounceInput");
  inputField.addEventListener("input",
debounce((e) => {
    console.log("User typed:",
e.target.value);
  }, 400));
</script>
```
Exercise 9 – Implement Throttle
Task: Write your own throttle function and use it to log scroll positions no more than once per second.

```
function throttle(func, limit) {
  let inThrottle;
  return function (...args) {
    if (!inThrottle) {
```

```
    func.apply(this, args);
    inThrottle = true;
    setTimeout(() => inThrottle = false,
limit);
    }
  };
}
window.addEventListener("scroll", throttle(()
=> {
  console.log("Scroll position:",
window.scrollY);
}, 1000));
```

Section 6: Additional Coding Exercises
Exercise 10 – Debug a Function
Task: Given a function that logs the square of a number, introduce a bug (e.g., using a wrong operator), then use debugging techniques to identify and fix the error.

```
function square(num) {
  // Intentional bug: using addition instead
of multiplication
  return num + num;
}
// Debug using console logs or breakpoints:
console.log("Square of 4 (buggy):",
square(4));
// Correct the function:
function correctSquare(num) {
  return num * num;
}
console.log("Square of 4 (correct):",
correctSquare(4));
```

Exercise 11 – Write a Simple Test Suite

Task: Create several test cases for a function `reverseString(str)` that reverses the given string. Use a simple assert function to log the results.

```
function reverseString(str) {
  return str.split('').reverse().join('');
}
function assertEqual(actual, expected,
testName) {
  if (actual === expected) {
    console.log(`PASSED [${testName}]`);
  } else {
    console.error(`FAILED [${testName}]:
Expected "${expected}", but got "${actual}"`);
  }
}
// Test cases:
assertEqual(reverseString("hello"), "olleh",
"reverseString should reverse 'hello'");
assertEqual(reverseString("JavaScript"),
"tpircSavaJ", "reverseString should reverse
'JavaScript'");
```

Exercise 12 – Create a Custom Logger with Levels

Task: Write a function `createLogger(level)` that returns an object with methods `info()`, `warn()`, and `error()`. Each method should log messages with a prefix corresponding to the level.

```
function createLogger(level) {
  return {
    info(message) {
      console.log(`[INFO] ${message}`);
    },
    warn(message) {
      console.warn(`[WARN] ${message}`);
```

```
    },
    error(message) {
      console.error(`[ERROR] ${message}`);
    }
  };
}
const logger = createLogger();
logger.info("This is an info message.");
logger.warn("This is a warning message.");
logger.error("This is an error message.");
```

Section 7: Multiple Choice Quiz – Debugging, Testing, and Best Practices

Which method is commonly used to output debugging information in JavaScript?
A. console.log()
B. document.write()
C. window.alert()
D. debugger.log()
Correct Answer: A
What does the debugger statement do in your code?
A. It logs an error message.
B. It halts execution so you can inspect variables.
C. It automatically fixes bugs.
D. It clears the console.
Correct Answer: B
Which block is used to handle errors in JavaScript?
A. try/catch
B. if/else
C. for/while
D. switch/case
Correct Answer: A

In a try/catch block, where is the error object available?
A. In the try block
B. In the catch block
C. Globally
D. Nowhere
Correct Answer: B

What is the purpose of using assertions in testing?
A. To slow down the code
B. To check if a value meets the expected result
C. To replace debugging
D. To deploy code
Correct Answer: B

Which tool is used to automatically check code for style and errors?
A. Webpack
B. Babel
C. ESLint
D. Node.js
Correct Answer: C

Debouncing a function helps to:
A. Execute the function immediately
B. Prevent the function from being called too frequently
C. Increase the function's speed
D. Call the function only once
Correct Answer: B

Throttling a function ensures that it is called:
A. Only after a delay
B. As many times as possible
C. At most once in a specified time period
D. Immediately without delay
Correct Answer: C

What is a common benefit of unit testing?
A. It makes your code run faster
B. It helps ensure each part of your code works as expected
C. It eliminates the need for debugging
D. It removes the need for error handling
Correct Answer: B

Which statement best describes linting?
A. Converting code to machine language
B. Automatically formatting code for consistency
C. Checking code for errors and enforcing coding standards
D. Minifying code for production
Correct Answer: C

What is the purpose of using try/catch in asynchronous code
with async/await?
A. To pause code execution
B. To handle errors gracefully
C. To speed up execution
D. To log successful operations
Correct Answer: B

Which method is used to log errors to the console?
A. console.log()
B. console.error()
C. console.info()
D. console.warn()
Correct Answer: B

Which of the following is NOT a benefit of following coding
best practices?
A. Improved code readability
B. Easier maintenance
C. Increased likelihood of bugs
D. Better collaboration among developers
Correct Answer: C

What does ESLint do when it finds a violation of a style rule?
A. Automatically corrects the code
B. Reports an error or warning
C. Stops code execution
D. Deletes the offending code
Correct Answer: B
Which of the following techniques helps in reducing the number of times an event handler is executed during rapid events like scrolling?
A. Debouncing
B. Recursion
C. Throttling
D. Both A and C
Correct Answer: D

Which is NOT a recommended practice for debugging?
A. Using console logs to inspect variables
B. Removing all error handling to speed up debugging
C. Setting breakpoints in developer tools
D. Writing small, testable code segments
Correct Answer: B

Recap & Next Steps

In this chapter, you learned how to effectively debug your code using logging and breakpoints, handle errors gracefully with try/catch blocks, write simple unit tests to validate your code, and follow best practices with linting and performance optimizations. These skills are essential for building reliable, maintainable, and efficient JavaScript applications.

Final Coding Tips
Break your code into small, testable functions and use assertions to verify their behavior.

Use debouncing and throttling to optimize event-driven actions.

Regularly run your linter and tests to catch issues early in the development cycle.

By working through the exercises and examples in this chapter, you're better prepared to build robust applications and maintain high code quality. In the next chapter, we'll dive into integrating third-party libraries, exploring advanced design patterns, or even building larger projects that combine everything you've learned.

Chapter 8: Modern JavaScript Modules, Third-Party Libraries, and Build Tools

Modern JavaScript development is built on the foundation of modular code, reusable libraries, and automated build tools. This chapter covers:

- Understanding Module Systems
- Package Management with npm
- Integrating Third-Party Libraries
- Setting Up a Build Process
- Mini Project: A Modular Date Formatter
- Additional Coding Exercises
- Multiple Choice Quiz

Section 1: Understanding Module Systems

JavaScript has evolved to support modules that help you organize and reuse your code. Two major module systems are commonly used:

ES6 Modules

ES6 modules allow you to export and import code using a standardized syntax.

Example – Exporting and Importing:

math.js
```
// Exporting functions from math.js
export function add(a, b) {
   return a + b;
}
export function multiply(a, b) {
   return a * b;
}
```

main.js
```
// Importing functions from math.js
import { add, multiply } from './math.js';
console.log("Add:", add(5, 3));          //
Output: 8
console.log("Multiply:", multiply(5, 3)); //
Output: 15
```

CommonJS Modules

Used primarily in Node.js, CommonJS modules use `require()` and `module.exports`.

Example – Exporting and Importing:

stringUtil.js
```
// Exporting functions using CommonJS syntax
function toUpperCase(str) {
   return str.toUpperCase();
}
function toLowerCase(str) {
   return str.toLowerCase();
}
module.exports = { toUpperCase, toLowerCase };
```

app.js
```
// Importing functions with CommonJS
const { toUpperCase, toLowerCase } =
require('./stringUtil');
console.log("Uppercase:",
toUpperCase("hello")); // Output: HELLO
console.log("Lowercase:",
toLowerCase("WORLD")); // Output: world
```

Section 2: Package Management with npm

npm (Node Package Manager) is the standard tool for managing third-party packages in JavaScript projects.

Key Concepts

package.json: Holds metadata and dependencies for your project.

Installing Packages: Use commands like npm install package-name to add libraries.

Local vs. Global Packages: Local packages are project-specific, while global packages are installed system-wide.

Code Example

Run the following commands in your terminal:
```
# Initialize a new project
npm init -y
# Install Lodash as a dependency
npm install lodash
```

Using Lodash in your code:
```
// Importing Lodash (using ES6 modules syntax,
if supported)
import _ from 'lodash';
```

```
const numbers = [10, 5, 8, 1];
const maxNumber = _.max(numbers);
console.log("Max number:", maxNumber); //
Output: 10
```

Section 3: Integrating Third-Party Libraries

Third-party libraries like Lodash, Moment.js, or Axios can greatly simplify your coding tasks.

Example – Using Moment.js

Install Moment.js:
```
npm install moment
```

Using Moment.js in your code:
```
import moment from 'moment';
const now = moment().format('MMMM Do YYYY,
h:mm:ss a');
console.log("Current date and time:", now);
```

Example – Using Lodash for Data Manipulation
```
import _ from 'lodash';
const users = [
  { name: 'Alice', age: 28 },
  { name: 'Bob', age: 22 },
  { name: 'Charlie', age: 35 }
];
const sortedUsers = _.sortBy(users, ['age']);
console.log("Users sorted by age:",
sortedUsers);
```

Section 4: Setting Up a Build Process

Modern projects often use build tools to bundle, transpile, and optimize your code. Webpack and Babel are popular choices.

Webpack Basics

Webpack bundles your modules into one or more files for the browser.

Example – Basic Webpack Configuration (webpack.config.js):

```
const path = require('path');
module.exports = {
  entry: './src/main.js', // your main file
  output: {
    filename: 'bundle.js',
    path: path.resolve(__dirname, 'dist')
  },
  module: {
    rules: [
      {
        test: /\.js$/,
        exclude: /node_modules/,
        use: {
          loader: 'babel-loader' // Transpile
ES6+ to ES5
        }
      }
    ]
  },
  mode: 'development'
};
```

Babel for Transpiling

Babel converts modern JavaScript into backward-compatible versions.

Example – Babel Configuration (.babelrc):

```
{
  "presets": ["@babel/preset-env"]
}
```

After setting up Webpack and Babel, run the build process with:

```
npx webpack
```

Section 5: Mini Project – A Modular Date Formatter

In this mini project, you will build a simple date formatter application that uses ES6 modules, Moment.js, and Lodash.

Project Overview

Modules: Split functionality into modules (e.g., formatting, utility functions).

Third-Party Libraries: Use Moment.js to format dates and Lodash for any helper functions.

Build Process: Bundle your code with Webpack.

Project Structure

```
project/
├── dist/
│   └── bundle.js
├── src/
│   ├── dateFormatter.js
│   ├── utils.js
│   └── main.js
├── package.json
├── webpack.config.js
└── .babelrc
```

Code Examples

src/dateFormatter.js
```
import moment from 'moment';
export function formatDate(date) {
  return moment(date).format('dddd, MMMM Do
YYYY, h:mm:ss a');
}
```

src/utils.js
```
import _ from 'lodash';
export function capitalizeWords(str) {
  return _.startCase(_.toLower(str));
}
```

src/main.js
```
import { formatDate } from
'./dateFormatter.js';
import { capitalizeWords } from './utils.js';
const date = new Date();
console.log("Formatted Date:",
formatDate(date));
const title = "hello world from modular
javascript";
console.log("Capitalized:",
capitalizeWords(title));
```

After writing your code, build your project using Webpack and open the generated *bundle.js* in your HTML file.

Section 6: Additional Coding Exercises

Exercise 1 – Create a Module for Math Utilities

Task: Create a module mathUtils.js that exports functions for add, subtract, and divide. Then, import these functions in a main file and log their outputs.

```
// mathUtils.js
```

```
export function add(a, b) {
  return a + b;
}
export function subtract(a, b) {
  return a - b;
}
export function divide(a, b) {
  if (b === 0) throw new Error("Division by
zero");
  return a / b;
}
```

Exercise 2 – Use a Third-Party Library

Task: Install the axios library via npm, then write a module that fetches data from an API endpoint (e.g., https://jsonplaceholder.typicode.com/todos/1) and logs the result.

```
// api.js
import axios from 'axios';
export async function fetchTodo() {
  try {
    const response = await
axios.get('https://jsonplaceholder.typicode.co
m/todos/1');
    console.log("Fetched Todo:",
response.data);
  } catch (error) {
    console.error("Error fetching todo:",
error);
  }
}
```

Exercise 3 – Create a Custom Babel Plugin (Conceptual)

Task: Research and write a brief explanation (in code comments) of what a Babel plugin does and give a simple example snippet (no need for a full implementation).

```
// A Babel plugin transforms JavaScript code
during the build process.
// For example, a plugin might convert custom
syntax into standard JavaScript.
// Here's a conceptual snippet:
module.exports = function(babel) {
  const { types: t } = babel;
  return {
    visitor: {
      Identifier(path) {
        // Example: rename all identifiers
'oldName' to 'newName'
        if (path.node.name === 'oldName') {
          path.node.name = 'newName';
        }
      }
    }
  };
};
```

Exercise 4 – Configure ESLint for Modules

Task: Create a sample .eslintrc.json configuration that enforces ES6 module syntax and import order.

```
{
  "env": {
    "browser": true,
    "es6": true
  },
  "extends": "eslint:recommended",
  "parserOptions": {
    "sourceType": "module"
```

```
  },
  "rules": {
    "indent": ["error", 2],
    "quotes": ["error", "single"],
    "semi": ["error", "always"],
    "import/order": ["error", {
      "groups": ["builtin", "external",
"internal"],
      "alphabetize": { "order": "asc",
"caseInsensitive": true }
    }]
  }
}
```

Exercise 5 – Create a Build Script

Task: Write an npm script in your `package.json` to run Webpack in development mode.

```
// In package.json:
"scripts": {
  "build": "webpack --mode development"
}
```

Section 7: Multiple Choice Quiz

What is the primary benefit of using ES6 modules?
A. They eliminate the need for build tools
B. They allow for better code organization and reusability
C. They run faster than CommonJS modules
D. They are supported in all browsers without transpilation
Correct Answer: B
Which command is used to install a package using npm?
A. npm init
B. npm start
C. npm install package-name
D. npm run package
Correct Answer: C

What file contains metadata and dependency information for a JavaScript project?
A. webpack.config.js
B. .babelrc
C. package.json
D. index.html
Correct Answer: C

Which of the following is a bundler that can be used with JavaScript projects?
A. Babel
B. Webpack
C. ESLint
D. npm
Correct Answer: B

What is the purpose of Babel in a modern JavaScript build process?
A. To bundle multiple files into one
B. To transpile modern JavaScript into backward-compatible code
C. To manage project dependencies
D. To lint code for style errors
Correct Answer: B

Which syntax is used to import a default export from an ES6 module?
A. import { default } from 'module';
B. import default from 'module';
C. import module from 'module';
D. import anyName from 'module';
Correct Answer: D

In CommonJS modules, which function is used to export functionality?
A. export
B. module.exports
C. define
D. require
Correct Answer: B

Which of the following tools is used to manage third-party packages in JavaScript?

A. npm

B. Webpack

C. Babel

D. ESLint

Correct Answer: A

What does the following Webpack configuration property define?

```
output: {
    filename: 'bundle.js'
}
```

A. The name of the entry file

B. The name of the output file after bundling

C. The folder where modules are located

D. The configuration for Babel

Correct Answer: B

Which statement best describes a module in JavaScript?

A. A block of code that executes automatically on page load

B. A reusable piece of code that exports and imports functionality

C. A function that handles asynchronous events

D. A configuration file for build tools

Correct Answer: B

How can you ensure that your modern JavaScript code runs in older browsers?

A. Use ES6 modules without transpilation

B. Transpile your code using Babel

C. Avoid using any third-party libraries

D. Write all code in ES5

Correct Answer: B

What is the purpose of a bundler like Webpack?
A. To create individual files for each module
B. To merge all your JavaScript modules into a single or few files
C. To directly run code in the browser without build steps
D. To replace npm for package management
Correct Answer: B

Which file is used to configure Babel?
A. webpack.config.js
B. .babelrc
C. package.json
D. babel.config.js
Correct Answer: B

What does the import statement do in an ES6 module?
A. It exports functions from a module
B. It imports functionality from another module
C. It initializes the project
D. It creates a new module
Correct Answer: B

Which of the following is NOT a benefit of using a build tool?
A. Code optimization and minification
B. Transpiling modern JavaScript for older browsers
C. Automatic dependency management
D. Running code without a browser
Correct Answer: D

How would you write an npm script to run Webpack in production mode?
A. "build": "webpack --mode development"
B. "build": "webpack --mode production"
C. "start": "webpack --mode production"
D. "prod": "webpack --env production"
Correct Answer: B

Recap & Next Steps

In this chapter, you learned how to structure your code using modules, manage your project dependencies with npm, integrate powerful third-party libraries, and set up a modern build process with tools like Webpack and Babel. These techniques help you write scalable, maintainable code and prepare your projects for production.

Final Coding Tip

As you integrate modules and third-party libraries, keep your code organized by separating concerns into different files and always use a build process to ensure your code is optimized and compatible across different environments.

By working through these detailed examples, exercises, and quiz questions, you're now better equipped to manage modern JavaScript projects. In the next chapter, we might explore advanced design patterns, state management, or even dive into frameworks to further enhance your development toolkit.

Chapter 9: Advanced Design Patterns and Functional Programming

Modern JavaScript development benefits greatly from both functional programming and well-established design patterns. These techniques can help you organize your code, reduce side effects, and create highly reusable components.

Section 1: Introduction to Functional Programming

Functional programming (FP) emphasizes writing pure functions, avoiding shared state, and using functions as first-class citizens. Key concepts include:

Pure Functions: Functions that return the same output for the same input and do not cause side effects.

Immutability: Once data is created, it is not modified. Higher-Order Functions: Functions that take other functions as arguments or return functions.

Function Composition: Combining simple functions to build more complex ones.

Code Examples

Example 1 – Pure Function & Immutability:
```
// Pure function that adds two numbers
function add(a, b) {
   return a + b;
}
console.log(add(2, 3)); // Output: 5
// Immutability: Instead of modifying an
array, return a new one
const numbers = [1, 2, 3];
const newNumbers = [...numbers, 4]; // New
array with 4 added
console.log("Original:", numbers);   // [1, 2,
3]
console.log("New:", newNumbers);       // [1,
2, 3, 4]
```

Example 2 – Higher-Order Functions (map, filter, reduce):
```
const nums = [1, 2, 3, 4, 5];
// Using map to create a new array with
squared numbers
const squares = nums.map(num => num * num);
```

```
console.log("Squares:", squares); // [1, 4, 9,
16, 25]
// Using filter to get even numbers
const evens = nums.filter(num => num % 2 ===
0);
console.log("Evens:", evens); // [2, 4]
// Using reduce to sum numbers
const sum = nums.reduce((total, num) => total
+ num, 0);
console.log("Sum:", sum); // 15
```

Coding Exercises
Exercise 1 – Write a Pure Function
Task: Create a pure function `multiply` that takes two numbers and returns their product without modifying any external variable.

```
function multiply(a, b) {
   return a * b;
}
console.log("Multiply 3 * 4 =", multiply(3,
4)); // Expected: 12
```

Exercise 2 – Immutably Update an Array
Task: Write a function `addItem` that takes an array and an item, and returns a new array with the item appended (without modifying the original array).

```
function addItem(arr, item) {
   return [...arr, item];
}
const original = [1, 2, 3];
const updated = addItem(original, 4);
console.log("Original:", original); // [1, 2,
3]
console.log("Updated:", updated);   // [1, 2,
3, 4]
```

Exercise 3 – Compose Functions

Task: Create two functions: `double(num)` that doubles a number, and `increment(num)` that adds one. Then write a function `compose` that takes two functions and returns their composition.

```
const double = num => num * 2;
const increment = num => num + 1;
const compose = (f, g) => x => f(g(x));
const doubleAfterIncrement = compose(double,
increment);
console.log(doubleAfterIncrement(3)); // (3 +
1) * 2 = 8
```

Exercise 4 – Filter and Map

Task: Given an array of numbers, use a combination of `filter` and `map` to first filter out odd numbers and then square the remaining even numbers.

```
const numbers = [1, 2, 3, 4, 5, 6];
const evenSquares = numbers.filter(n => n % 2
=== 0).map(n => n * n);
console.log("Even Squares:", evenSquares); //
[4, 16, 36]
```

Section 2: Classic Design Patterns in JavaScript

Design patterns provide time-proven solutions to common problems. We'll explore a few that are especially useful in JavaScript.

Singleton Pattern

Ensures a class has only one instance and provides a global point of access.

Example – Singleton:

```javascript
const Singleton = (function() {
  let instance;
  function createInstance() {
    return { name: "Singleton Instance" };
  }
  return {
    getInstance() {
      if (!instance) {
        instance = createInstance();
      }
      return instance;
    }
  };
})();
const s1 = Singleton.getInstance();
const s2 = Singleton.getInstance();
console.log("Same instance?", s1 === s2); //
true
```

Factory Pattern

Creates objects without exposing the creation logic.

Example – Factory:
```javascript
function carFactory(make, model) {
  return {
    make,
    model,
    drive() {
      console.log(`${make} ${model} is
driving.`);
    }
  };
}
const car1 = carFactory("Toyota", "Corolla");
```

```
car1.drive(); // Output: Toyota Corolla is
driving.
```

Observer Pattern

Defines a subscription mechanism to notify multiple objects about events.

Example – Observer:
```
class Subject {
  constructor() {
    this.observers = [];
  }
  subscribe(observer) {
    this.observers.push(observer);
  }
  unsubscribe(observer) {
    this.observers = this.observers.filter(obs
=> obs !== observer);
  }
  notify(data) {
    this.observers.forEach(observer =>
observer.update(data));
  }
}
class Observer {
  constructor(name) {
    this.name = name;
  }
  update(data) {
    console.log(`${this.name} received update:
${data}`);
  }
}
const subject = new Subject();
const observer1 = new Observer("Observer 1");
```

```
const observer2 = new Observer("Observer 2");
subject.subscribe(observer1);
subject.subscribe(observer2);
subject.notify("New Event Occurred");
// Output: Observer 1 received update: New
Event Occurred
//          Observer 2 received update: New
Event Occurred
```

Coding Exercises
Exercise 5 – Implement a Singleton
Task: Write your own singleton pattern for a configuration object that stores settings.

```
const ConfigSingleton = (function() {
  let instance;
  function createInstance() {
    return { apiUrl:
"https://api.example.com", timeout: 5000 };
  }
  return {
    getInstance() {
      if (!instance) {
        instance = createInstance();
      }
      return instance;
    }
  };
})();
const config1 = ConfigSingleton.getInstance();
const config2 = ConfigSingleton.getInstance();
console.log("Configs are same?", config1 ===
config2); // Expected: true
```

Exercise 6 – Build a Factory Function

Task: Create a factory function `createUser` that returns user objects with properties `name` and `role` and a method `describe()`.

```
function createUser(name, role) {
  return {
    name,
    role,
    describe() {
      console.log(`${this.name} is a
${this.role}`);
    }
  };
}
const user1 = createUser("Alice", "Admin");
user1.describe(); // Output: Alice is a Admin
```

Exercise 7 – Observer Pattern Practice

Task: Implement a simple observer pattern where a subject notifies its observers whenever a counter is incremented.

```
class Counter {
  constructor() {
    this.count = 0;
    this.observers = [];
  }
  subscribe(observer) {
    this.observers.push(observer);
  }
  increment() {
    this.count++;
    this.notify();
  }
  notify() {
    this.observers.forEach(observer =>
observer.update(this.count));
```

```
  }
}
class Display {
  update(count) {
    console.log(`Counter updated: ${count}`);
  }
}
const counter = new Counter();
const display = new Display();
counter.subscribe(display);
counter.increment(); // Output: Counter
updated: 1
counter.increment(); // Output: Counter
updated: 2
```

Section 3: Functional Design Patterns

Functional design patterns such as currying, partial application, and memoization can make your code more efficient and reusable.

Currying

Transform a function that takes multiple arguments into a sequence of functions that each take a single argument.

Example – Currying:
```
function curryAdd(a) {
  return function(b) {
    return a + b;
  };
}
const addFive = curryAdd(5);
console.log(addFive(10)); // Output: 15
```

Partial Application

Pre-fill some arguments of a function to create a new function.

Example – Partial Application:
```
function greet(greeting, name) {
   return `${greeting}, ${name}!`;
}
const sayHello = greet.bind(null, "Hello");
console.log(sayHello("Bob")); // Output:
Hello, Bob!
```

Memoization

Cache the results of function calls to improve performance on expensive operations.

Example – Memoization:
```
function memoize(fn) {
   const cache = {};
   return function(...args) {
     const key = JSON.stringify(args);
     if (cache[key]) {
       return cache[key];
     }
     const result = fn(...args);
     cache[key] = result;
     return result;
   };
}
function fibonacci(n) {
   if (n < 2) return n;
   return fibonacci(n - 1) + fibonacci(n - 2);
}
const memoizedFibonacci = memoize(fibonacci);
console.log(memoizedFibonacci(10)); // Fast
calculation of the 10th Fibonacci number
```

Coding Exercises

Exercise 8 – Implement Currying
Task: Create a curried function for concatenating three strings.

```
function curriedConcat(a) {
  return function(b) {
    return function(c) {
      return a + b + c;
    };
  };
}
const concatWithHello = curriedConcat("Hello,
")("my name is ");
console.log(concatWithHello("Alice")); //
Output: Hello, my name is Alice
```

Exercise 9 – Partial Application Challenge
Task: Write a function multiplyThree that multiplies three numbers. Then create a partially applied function doubleAndMultiply that fixes the first argument as 2.

```
function multiplyThree(a, b, c) {
  return a * b * c;
}
const doubleAndMultiply =
multiplyThree.bind(null, 2);
console.log(doubleAndMultiply(3, 4)); //
Expected: 2 * 3 * 4 = 24
```

Exercise 10 – Memoize a Recursive Function
Task: Use memoization to optimize a recursive factorial function.

```
function factorial(n) {
  if (n <= 1) return 1;
  return n * factorial(n - 1);
}
const memoizedFactorial = memoize(factorial);
```

```
console.log("Factorial of 5:",
memoizedFactorial(5)); // Output: 120
```

Section 4: Mini Project – Functional Todo App

In this mini project, build a simple Todo application using functional programming principles and design patterns.

Project Overview
Pure Functions: Write functions to add, remove, and list todos.

Immutability: Return new arrays when updating the list. Design Patterns: Use a factory function to create Todo items and higher-order functions to manage state.

Code Example
```
// Todo factory function (pure)
function createTodo(title) {
   return { title, completed: false };
}
// Pure function to add a todo (returns a new
list)
function addTodo(list, todo) {
   return [...list, todo];
}
// Pure function to remove a todo by title
function removeTodo(list, title) {
   return list.filter(todo => todo.title !==
title);
}
// Pure function to mark a todo as completed
function completeTodo(list, title) {
   return list.map(todo =>
     todo.title === title ? { ...todo,
completed: true } : todo
```

```
  );
}
// Initial state
let todos = [];
// Simulate adding todos
todos = addTodo(todos, createTodo("Learn
JavaScript"));
todos = addTodo(todos, createTodo("Practice
Functional Programming"));
console.log("Todos after adding:", todos);
// Complete a todo
todos = completeTodo(todos, "Learn
JavaScript");
console.log("Todos after completing:", todos);
// Remove a todo
todos = removeTodo(todos, "Practice Functional
Programming");
console.log("Todos after removal:", todos);
```

Coding Exercise
Exercise 11 – Extend the Todo App
Task: Add a function listTodos that logs all todos with their
status in a formatted string.

```
function listTodos(list) {
  list.forEach((todo, index) => {
    console.log(`${index + 1}. ${todo.title} -
${todo.completed ? "Completed" :
"Incomplete"}`);
  });
}
listTodos(todos);
```

Section 5: Additional Coding Exercises

Exercise 12 – Pure Function Challenge

Task: Write a function that takes an array of numbers and returns a new array with each number doubled, without modifying the original array.

```
function doubleNumbers(arr) {
   return arr.map(num => num * 2);
}
const nums = [1, 2, 3];
console.log("Doubled:", doubleNumbers(nums));
// [2, 4, 6]
```

Exercise 13 – Observer with Functional Approach

Task: Implement a simple observer mechanism using pure functions. Create a function createNotifier that maintains a list of subscribers and notifies them when called.

```
function createNotifier() {
   let subscribers = [];
   return {
     subscribe(fn) {
       subscribers.push(fn);
     },
     notify(message) {
       subscribers.forEach(fn => fn(message));
     }
   };
}
const notifier = createNotifier();
notifier.subscribe(msg =>
console.log("Subscriber 1:", msg));
notifier.subscribe(msg =>
console.log("Subscriber 2:", msg));
notifier.notify("Hello Observers!");
```

Exercise 14 - Factory Function for Settings

Task: Write a factory function `createSettings` that returns an object with default settings. Allow overriding defaults by passing an options object.

```
function createSettings(options = {}) {
  const defaults = { theme: "light",
notifications: true, version: "1.0.0" };
  return { ...defaults, ...options };
}
const userSettings = createSettings({ theme:
"dark" });
console.log("User Settings:", userSettings);
```

Section 6: Multiple Choice Quiz

What is a pure function in functional programming?
A. A function that modifies external state
B. A function that always returns the same output for the same input and has no side effects
C. A function that only uses global variables
D. A function that runs asynchronously
Correct Answer: B

Which of the following is a benefit of immutability?
A. Easier to track changes over time
B. Reduced chance of side effects
C. Better for debugging and testing
D. All of the above
Correct Answer: D

What does the term "higher-order function" mean?
A. A function that returns a function or takes a function as an argument
B. A function that runs at a higher priority
C. A function that can only be used once
D. A function that is defined globally
Correct Answer: A

In currying, a function is transformed into a sequence of functions that each take:
A. No arguments
B. A single argument
C. Multiple arguments
D. An object
Correct Answer: B

Which design pattern ensures a class has only one instance?
A. Factory Pattern
B. Observer Pattern
C. Singleton Pattern
D. Decorator Pattern
Correct Answer: C

What is the main purpose of the Factory Pattern?
A. To enforce a single instance
B. To create objects without exposing the instantiation logic
C. To observe state changes
D. To bind functions to a context
Correct Answer: B

The Observer Pattern is used to:
A. Create objects from a common blueprint
B. Notify multiple subscribers of state changes
C. Compose multiple functions
D. Cache the results of function calls
Correct Answer: B

What is memoization?
A. A technique to delay function execution
B. A technique to cache the results of function calls
C. A method of function currying
D. A way to convert asynchronous code to synchronous
Correct Answer: B

Which of the following best describes function composition?
A. Writing a single function that does everything
B. Combining multiple functions such that the output of one is the input of the next
C. Converting a function to an arrow function
D. Splitting a function into smaller functions without any connection
Correct Answer: B

What is partial application?
A. Pre-filling some arguments of a function to create a new function
B. Splitting a function into two parts
C. Returning a function without executing it
D. A way to bind a function's this value
Correct Answer: A

A curried function:
A. Takes an object and returns an array
B. Breaks a function with multiple arguments into a series of unary functions
C. Immediately executes all functions
D. Requires binding of the this keyword
Correct Answer: B

In a functional Todo app, why is immutability important?
A. It allows direct modification of the state
B. It ensures that each update returns a new state, making debugging easier
C. It slows down the application
D. It requires less memory
Correct Answer: B

Which of the following is NOT typically associated with functional programming?
A. Side effects
B. Pure functions
C. Immutability
D. Higher-order functions
Correct Answer: A

What does the spread operator (...) help with in the context of immutability?

A. Modifying the original array

B. Creating shallow copies of arrays or objects

C. Deep cloning objects automatically

D. Binding functions

Correct Answer: B

Which pattern is especially useful for managing state updates in a predictable manner?

A. Observer Pattern

B. Singleton Pattern

C. Functional Programming Paradigms

D. Module Pattern

Correct Answer: C

What is one advantage of using functional design patterns over imperative code?

A. They encourage side effects

B. They often result in shorter, more predictable code

C. They are harder to test

D. They require mutable state

Correct Answer: B

Recap & Next Steps

In this chapter, you explored advanced design patterns and functional programming techniques in JavaScript. You learned about pure functions, immutability, higher-order functions, currying, and memoization, and saw how classic design patterns like Singleton, Factory, and Observer can be implemented. By practicing these techniques in a mini project and through a series of exercises and quizzes, you now have powerful tools to write more modular, maintainable, and efficient code.

Final Coding Tip

Adopt a functional mindset by favoring pure functions and immutable data. Combine these with well-known design patterns to build scalable and testable applications. As you continue your journey, challenge yourself to refactor imperative code into a more functional style.

100 Bonus Code Snippets

Basics & Fundamentals

Hello, World!

```
// Exercise 1: Hello, World!
console.log("Hello, World!");
```

Personal Greeting

```
// Exercise 2: Personal Greeting
const myName = "Alice";
console.log(`Hello, my name is ${myName}!`);
```

Variable Declaration

```
// Exercise 3: Variable Declaration
const greeting = "Hi there!";
let age = 30;
var isStudent = false;
console.log(greeting, age, isStudent);
console.log(typeof greeting, typeof age,
typeof isStudent);
```

Arithmetic Operations

```
// Exercise 4: Arithmetic Operations
let a = 10, b = 3;
console.log("Sum:", a + b);
console.log("Difference:", a - b);
console.log("Product:", a * b);
console.log("Quotient:", a / b);
console.log("Remainder:", a % b);
```

Temperature Converter (Celsius to Fahrenheit)

```
// Exercise 5: Temperature Converter
let celsius = 25;
let fahrenheit = (celsius * 9/5) + 32;
```

```javascript
console.log(`${celsius}°C is
${fahrenheit}°F`);
```

Simple Input Simulation (Using prompt if available)

```javascript
// Exercise 6: Simple Input Simulation
(Uncomment if running in a browser)
// let userName = prompt("What is your
name?");
// console.log(`Hello, ${userName}!`);
```

Positive Number Checker

```javascript
// Exercise 7: Positive Number Checker
let num = 5;
if (num > 0) {
  console.log("Positive");
}
```

Even or Odd Checker

```javascript
// Exercise 8: Even or Odd Checker
let number = 8;
if (number % 2 === 0) {
  console.log("Even");
} else {
  console.log("Odd");
}
```

Grade Assigner

```javascript
// Exercise 9: Grade Assigner
let score = 85;
if (score >= 90) {
  console.log("Grade: A");
} else if (score >= 80) {
  console.log("Grade: B");
} else if (score >= 70) {
  console.log("Grade: C");
} else {
  console.log("Grade: D or below");
}
```

Day of the Week (Switch Statement)

```javascript
// Exercise 10: Day of the Week (Switch)
```

```
let day = "Tuesday";
switch(day) {
  case "Monday":
    console.log("It is Monday.");
    break;
  case "Tuesday":
    console.log("It is Tuesday.");
    break;
  case "Wednesday":
    console.log("It is Wednesday.");
    break;
  default:
    console.log("Another day.");
}
```

Control Structures & Functions

For Loop – Numbers 1 to 10

```
// Exercise 11: For Loop – Numbers 1 to 10
for (let i = 1; i <= 10; i++) {
  console.log(i);
}
```

While Loop – Numbers 1 to 10

```
// Exercise 12: While Loop – Numbers 1 to 10
let i = 1;
while (i <= 10) {
  console.log(i);
  i++;
}
```

Do-While Loop Example

```
// Exercise 13: Do-While Loop Example
let j = 1;
do {
  console.log(j);
  j++;
} while (j <= 10);
```

Sum of Numbers 1 to 100

```
// Exercise 14: Sum of Numbers 1 to 100
let sum = 0;
for (let i = 1; i <= 100; i++) {
  sum += i;
}
console.log("Sum from 1 to 100:", sum);
```

Multiplication Table (for 5)

```
// Exercise 15: Multiplication Table for 5
const base = 5;
for (let i = 1; i <= 10; i++) {
  console.log(`${base} x ${i} = ${base * i}`);
}
```

Square Function

```
// Exercise 16: Square Function
function square(num) {
  return num * num;
}
console.log("Square of 4:", square(4));
```

Cube Function

```
// Exercise 17: Cube Function
function cube(num) {
  return num * num * num;
}
console.log("Cube of 3:", cube(3));
```

Max of Two Numbers

```
// Exercise 18: Max of Two Numbers
function max(a, b) {
  return a > b ? a : b;
}
console.log("Max of 7 and 10:", max(7, 10));
```

Max in Array

```
// Exercise 19: Max in Array
function maxInArray(arr) {
  return Math.max(...arr);
}
```

```javascript
console.log("Max in array [3, 8, 1, 6]:",
maxInArray([3, 8, 1, 6]));
```

Min in Array

```javascript
// Exercise 20: Min in Array
function minInArray(arr) {
  return Math.min(...arr);
}
console.log("Min in array [3, 8, 1, 6]:",
minInArray([3, 8, 1, 6]));
```

Average Calculator

```javascript
// Exercise 21: Average Calculator
function average(arr) {
  let sum = arr.reduce((total, num) => total +
num, 0);
  return sum / arr.length;
}
console.log("Average of [2,4,6,8]:",
average([2, 4, 6, 8]));
```

String Reverser

```javascript
// Exercise 22: String Reverser
function reverseString(str) {
  return str.split('').reverse().join('');
}
console.log("Reverse of 'hello':",
reverseString("hello"));
```

Palindrome Checker

```javascript
// Exercise 23: Palindrome Checker
function isPalindrome(str) {
  const reversed =
str.split('').reverse().join('');
  return str === reversed;
}
console.log("Is 'racecar' a palindrome?",
isPalindrome("racecar"));
```

Factorial (Recursion)

```javascript
// Exercise 24: Factorial (Recursion)
```

```
function factorial(n) {
  if (n <= 1) return 1;
  return n * factorial(n - 1);
}
console.log("Factorial of 5:", factorial(5));
```

Fibonacci Sequence Generator

```
// Exercise 25: Fibonacci Sequence Generator
function fibonacci(n) {
  const seq = [0, 1];
  for (let i = 2; i < n; i++) {
    seq[i] = seq[i - 1] + seq[i - 2];
  }
  return seq;
}
console.log("First 10 Fibonacci numbers:",
fibonacci(10));
```

Arrow Function Addition

```
// Exercise 26: Arrow Function Addition
const add = (a, b) => a + b;
console.log("3 + 4 =", add(3, 4));
```

Template Literal Greeting

```
// Exercise 27: Template Literal Greeting
function greet(name) {
  console.log(`Hello, ${name}! Welcome to
JavaScript.`);
}
greet("Alice");
```

Callback Example with setTimeout

```
// Exercise 28: Callback Example
function doTask(callback) {
  setTimeout(() => {
    console.log("Task completed.");
    callback();
  }, 1000);
}
```

```
doTask(() => console.log("Callback
executed."));
```

Simple Callback Calculator

```
// Exercise 29: Simple Callback Calculator
function calculate(a, b, operation, callback)
{
  const result = operation(a, b);
  callback(result);
}
calculate(5, 3, (x, y) => x + y, (result) =>
console.log("Sum is:", result));
// Alternatively, using a defined operation:
function addOperation(x, y) { return x + y; }
calculate(5, 3, addOperation, (result) =>
console.log("Sum is:", result));
```

Immediately Invoked Function Expression (IIFE)

```
// Exercise 30: IIFE
(function() {
  console.log("IIFE executed");
})();
```

Arrays, Objects & Data Structures

Array of Fruits

```
// Exercise 31: Array of Fruits
const fruits = ["apple", "banana", "cherry",
"date", "elderberry"];
fruits.forEach(fruit => console.log(fruit));
```

Array Length

```
// Exercise 32: Array Length
const items = [1, 2, 3, 4, 5];
console.log("Array length:", items.length);
```

Modify Array Element

```
// Exercise 33: Modify Array Element
let numbers = [10, 20, 30, 40, 50];
numbers[2] = 35;
```

```
console.log("Updated numbers:", numbers);
```

Using push()

```
// Exercise 34: Using push()
let arr = [];
arr.push("first");
arr.push("second");
arr.push("third");
console.log("Array after push:", arr);
```

Using pop()

```
// Exercise 35: Using pop()
let arr2 = ["a", "b", "c", "d"];
arr2.pop();
console.log("Array after pop:", arr2);
```

Using splice() to Remove Element

```
// Exercise 36: Using splice() to Remove
Element
let cities = ["New York", "Los Angeles",
"Chicago", "Houston"];
const index = cities.indexOf("Chicago");
if (index !== -1) {
  cities.splice(index, 1);
}
console.log("Cities after removal:", cities);
```

Filter Even Numbers

```
// Exercise 37: Filter Even Numbers
const nums = [1, 2, 3, 4, 5, 6];
const evens = nums.filter(n => n % 2 === 0);
console.log("Even numbers:", evens);
```

Map for Squaring Numbers

```
// Exercise 38: Map for Squaring Numbers
const squares = nums.map(n => n * n);
console.log("Squares:", squares);
```

Reduce for Sum

```
// Exercise 39: Reduce for Sum
const total = nums.reduce((acc, curr) => acc +
curr, 0);
```

```
console.log("Sum of array:", total);
```

Sorting Strings

```
// Exercise 40: Sorting Strings
const names = ["Charlie", "Alice", "Bob"];
names.sort();
console.log("Sorted names:", names);
```

2D Array (Matrix) Creation

```
// Exercise 41: 2D Array (Matrix)
const matrix = [
  [1, 2, 3],
  [4, 5, 6],
  [7, 8, 9]
];
console.log("Matrix:", matrix);
```

Object Creation – Person

```
// Exercise 42: Object Creation – Person
const person = { name: "Alice", age: 30, city:
"Wonderland" };
console.log("Person:", person);
```

Access Object Properties

```
// Exercise 43: Access Object Properties
console.log("Name:", person.name);
console.log("Age:", person.age);
console.log("City:", person.city);
```

Add Property with Bracket Notation

```
// Exercise 44: Add Property with Bracket
Notation
person["occupation"] = "Adventurer";
console.log("Updated Person:", person);
```

Loop Through Object Properties

```
// Exercise 45: Loop Through Object Properties
for (let key in person) {
  console.log(`${key}: ${person[key]}`);
}
```

Array of Objects – Students

```
// Exercise 46: Array of Objects – Students
```

```javascript
const students = [
  { name: "Alice", grade: 90 },
  { name: "Bob", grade: 85 },
  { name: "Charlie", grade: 95 }
];
students.forEach(student =>
console.log(student.name));
```

Object.keys() Usage

```javascript
// Exercise 47: Object.keys() Usage
console.log("Keys:", Object.keys(person));
```

Object.values() Usage

```javascript
// Exercise 48: Object.values() Usage
console.log("Values:", Object.values(person));
```

Merge Two Objects

```javascript
// Exercise 49: Merge Two Objects
const obj1 = { a: 1, b: 2 };
const obj2 = { b: 3, c: 4 };
const merged = { ...obj1, ...obj2 };
console.log("Merged Object:", merged);
```

Object Destructuring

```javascript
// Exercise 50: Object Destructuring
const { name: personName, age: personAge } =
person;
console.log("Destructured:", personName,
personAge);
```

Closure – Counter Function

```javascript
// Exercise 51: Closure – Counter Function
function createCounter() {
  let count = 0;
  return function() {
    count++;
    return count;
  };
}
const counter = createCounter();
console.log(counter()); // 1
```

```
console.log(counter()); // 2
```
Secret Holder
```
// Exercise 52: Secret Holder
function createSecretHolder(secret) {
  return {
    getSecret() { return secret; },
    setSecret(newSecret) { secret = newSecret;
}
  };
}
const secretHolder =
createSecretHolder("mySecret");
console.log(secretHolder.getSecret());
secretHolder.setSecret("newSecret");
console.log(secretHolder.getSecret());
```
Array State via Closure
```
// Exercise 53: Array State via Closure
function createListManager() {
  const list = [];
  return {
    add(item) { list.push(item); },
    remove(item) {
      const index = list.indexOf(item);
      if (index > -1) list.splice(index, 1);
    },
    getList() { return [...list]; }
  };
}
const listManager = createListManager();
listManager.add("apple");
listManager.add("banana");
console.log(listManager.getList());
listManager.remove("apple");
console.log(listManager.getList());
```
Destructuring with Renaming
```
// Exercise 54: Destructuring with Renaming
```

```javascript
const car = { make: "Toyota", model:
"Corolla", year: 2020 };
const { make: carMake, model: carModel } =
car;
console.log(carMake, carModel);
```

Spread Operator for Array Copying

```javascript
// Exercise 55: Spread Operator for Array
Copying
const originalArray = [1, 2, 3];
const copiedArray = [...originalArray];
copiedArray.push(4);
console.log("Original:", originalArray);
console.log("Copied:", copiedArray);
```

DOM Manipulation & Event Handling

(Note: Some exercises require an HTML document. You can test these in a browser.)

Select Element by ID

```html
<!-- Exercise 56: Select Element by ID -->
<div id="myDiv">Hello!</div>
<script>
  const myDiv =
document.getElementById("myDiv");
  console.log(myDiv.textContent);
</script>
```

Select Element by Class

```html
<!-- Exercise 57: Select Element by Class -->
<p class="myClass">This is a paragraph.</p>
<script>
  const para =
document.querySelector(".myClass");
  para.textContent = "Updated text content.";
  console.log(para.textContent);
</script>
```

Create and Append Element

```
<!-- Exercise 58: Create and Append Element --
>
<script>
  const newPara = document.createElement("p");
  newPara.textContent = "This paragraph was
added dynamically.";
  document.body.appendChild(newPara);
</script>
```

Update Element Style

```
<!-- Exercise 59: Update Element Style -->
<p id="stylePara">Styled Text</p>
<script>
  const stylePara =
document.getElementById("stylePara");
  stylePara.style.color = "blue";
  stylePara.style.fontSize = "20px";
</script>
```

Button Click Event

```
<!-- Exercise 60: Button Click Event -->
<button id="clickButton">Click Me!</button>
<script>

document.getElementById("clickButton").addEven
tListener("click", () => {
    console.log("Button was clicked!");
  });
</script>
```

Dynamic List Creation

```
<!-- Exercise 61: Dynamic List Creation -->
<script>
  const ul = document.createElement("ul");
  ["Item 1", "Item 2", "Item
3"].forEach(itemText => {
    const li = document.createElement("li");
    li.textContent = itemText;
```

```
    ul.appendChild(li);
  });
  document.body.appendChild(ul);
</script>
```

Event Delegation

```
<!-- Exercise 62: Event Delegation -->
<ul id="delegatedList">
  <li>Item A</li>
  <li>Item B</li>
  <li>Item C</li>
</ul>
<script>

document.getElementById("delegatedList").addEv
entListener("click", function(event) {
    if (event.target.tagName === "LI") {
       console.log("Clicked item:",
event.target.textContent);
    }
  });
</script>
```

Toggle Class on Click

```
<!-- Exercise 63: Toggle Class on Click -->
<div id="toggleDiv">Toggle my class</div>
<button id="toggleButton">Toggle
Class</button>
<script>
  const toggleDiv =
document.getElementById("toggleDiv");

document.getElementById("toggleButton").addEve
ntListener("click", () => {
    toggleDiv.classList.toggle("active");
  });
</script>
<style>
```

```
.active { color: red; }
</style>
```

Form Submission Prevention

```html
<!-- Exercise 64: Form Submission Prevention -
->
<form id="myForm">
  <input type="text" id="nameInput"
placeholder="Enter name">
  <button type="submit">Submit</button>
</form>
<script>

document.getElementById("myForm").addEventList
ener("submit", function(e) {
    e.preventDefault();
    const name =
document.getElementById("nameInput").value;
    console.log("Form submitted with name:",
name);
  });
</script>
```

Change Image Source on Button Click

```html
<!-- Exercise 65: Change Image Source on
Button Click -->
<img id="myImage"
src="https://via.placeholder.com/150"
alt="Placeholder">
<button id="changeImage">Change Image</button>
<script>

document.getElementById("changeImage").addEven
tListener("click", () => {
    document.getElementById("myImage").src =
"https://via.placeholder.com/200";
  });
</script>
```

Input Event Listener

```html
<!-- Exercise 66: Input Event Listener -->
<input type="text" id="inputField"
placeholder="Type here...">
<script>

document.getElementById("inputField").addEvent
Listener("input", function(e) {
    console.log("Current input:",
e.target.value);
  });
</script>
```

Hover Effect with Mouse Events

```html
<!-- Exercise 67: Hover Effect with Mouse
Events -->
<div id="hoverDiv">Hover over me</div>
<script>
  const hoverDiv =
document.getElementById("hoverDiv");
  hoverDiv.addEventListener("mouseover", () =>
hoverDiv.style.color = "green");
  hoverDiv.addEventListener("mouseout", () =>
hoverDiv.style.color = "black");
</script>
```

Using innerHTML

```html
<!-- Exercise 68: Using innerHTML -->
<div id="htmlDiv"></div>
<script>
  document.getElementById("htmlDiv").innerHTML
= "<strong>Bold Text</strong> inside a div.";
</script>
```

Remove Element on Right-Click

```html
<!-- Exercise 69: Remove Element on Right-
Click -->
<p id="removePara">Right-click me to remove
me.</p>
```

```
<script>

document.getElementById("removePara").addEvent
Listener("contextmenu", function(e) {
    e.preventDefault();
    this.remove();
  });
</script>
```

Simple To-Do List

```
<!-- Exercise 70: Simple To-Do List -->
<h3>My To-Do List</h3>
<input type="text" id="todoInput"
placeholder="New to-do">
<button id="addTodo">Add To-Do</button>
<ul id="todoList"></ul>
<script>
  const todoInput =
document.getElementById("todoInput");
  const todoList =
document.getElementById("todoList");

document.getElementById("addTodo").addEventLis
tener("click", () => {
    const text = todoInput.value.trim();
    if (text !== "") {
      const li = document.createElement("li");
      li.textContent = text;
      // Remove item on click
      li.addEventListener("click", () =>
li.remove());
      todoList.appendChild(li);
      todoInput.value = "";
    }
  });
</script>
```

Asynchronous Programming & APIs

setTimeout Example

```
// Exercise 71: setTimeout Example
setTimeout(() => console.log("This message is
delayed by 2 seconds."), 2000);
```

Promise Creation

```
// Exercise 72: Promise Creation
const promiseExample = new Promise((resolve,
reject) => {
  setTimeout(() => resolve("Promise
resolved!"), 1000);
});
promiseExample.then(message =>
console.log(message));
```

Promise Rejection Handling

```
// Exercise 73: Promise Rejection Handling
const promiseReject = new Promise((resolve,
reject) => {
  setTimeout(() => reject("Promise
rejected!"), 1000);
});
promiseReject.catch(error =>
console.error(error));
```

Async/Await Example

```
// Exercise 74: Async/Await Example
async function asyncExample() {
  const message = await promiseExample;
  console.log("Async/Await:", message);
}
asyncExample();
```

Try/Catch in Async Function

```
// Exercise 75: Try/Catch in Async Function
async function asyncWithError() {
  try {
    const result = await promiseReject;
    console.log(result);
```

```
  } catch (error) {
    console.error("Caught error:", error);
  }
}
asyncWithError();
```

Fetch API Request

```
// Exercise 76: Fetch API Request
async function fetchTodo() {
  try {
    const response = await
fetch("https://jsonplaceholder.typicode.com/to
dos/1");
    const todo = await response.json();
    console.log("Todo title:", todo.title);
  } catch (error) {
    console.error("Fetch error:", error);
  }
}
fetchTodo();
```

Fetch Error Handling

```
// Exercise 77: Fetch Error Handling
async function fetchInvalid() {
  try {
    const response = await
fetch("https://jsonplaceholder.typicode.com/in
validurl");
    if (!response.ok) throw new Error("Network
response not ok");
    const data = await response.json();
    console.log(data);
  } catch (error) {
    console.error("Handled fetch error:",
error);
  }
}
fetchInvalid();
```

Promise.all Usage

```
// Exercise 78: Promise.all Usage
const promise1 = new Promise(resolve =>
setTimeout(() => resolve("First"), 1000));
const promise2 = new Promise(resolve =>
setTimeout(() => resolve("Second"), 1500));
Promise.all([promise1, promise2]).then(results
=> console.log("Promise.all results:",
results));
```

Promise.race Usage

```
// Exercise 79: Promise.race Usage
const promiseA = new Promise(resolve =>
setTimeout(() => resolve("Fast"), 1000));
const promiseB = new Promise(resolve =>
setTimeout(() => resolve("Slow"), 3000));
Promise.race([promiseA, promiseB]).then(result
=> console.log("Promise.race result:",
result));
```

Simulate Delayed Greeting

```
// Exercise 80: Simulate Delayed Greeting
function delayedGreeting() {
  return new Promise(resolve => {
    setTimeout(() => resolve("Hello after 2
seconds!"), 2000);
  });
}
async function greet() {
  const greeting = await delayedGreeting();
  console.log(greeting);
}
greet();
```

Advanced Concepts – Closures, Prototypes, & Classes

Closure – Increment Counter

```
// Exercise 81: Closure - Increment Counter
function counter() {
  let count = 0;
  return function() {
    return ++count;
  };
}
const c = counter();
console.log(c()); // 1
console.log(c()); // 2
```

Secret Holder with Closure
(Similar to Exercise 52 above)

Arrow Function vs. Regular Function (this context)

```
// Exercise 83: Arrow Function vs. Regular
Function
const obj = {
  value: 42,
  regular: function() {
    console.log("Regular function
this.value:", this.value);
  },
  arrow: () => {
    console.log("Arrow function this.value:",
this.value);
  }
};
obj.regular(); // 42
obj.arrow();    // undefined (or global value)
```

call() to Set this

```
// Exercise 84: call() to Set this
function showName() {
  console.log("My name is", this.name);
}
const user = { name: "Bob" };
```

```
showName.call(user);
```

bind() to Preserve this

```
// Exercise 85: bind() to Preserve this
const counterObj = {
  count: 0,
  increment() {
    this.count++;
    console.log(this.count);
  }
};
const unbound = counterObj.increment;
const bound = unbound.bind(counterObj);
bound(); // 1
bound(); // 2
```

Constructor Function & Prototype Method

```
// Exercise 86: Constructor Function &
Prototype Method
function Animal(name) {
  this.name = name;
}
Animal.prototype.speak = function() {
  console.log(`${this.name} makes a sound.`);
};
const dog = new Animal("Rex");
dog.speak();
```

Object.create() Example

```
// Exercise 87: Object.create() Example
const animalProto = {
  speak() {
    console.log(`${this.name} speaks.`);
  }
};
const cat = Object.create(animalProto);
cat.name = "Whiskers";
cat.speak();
```

ES6 Class – Basic Usage

```javascript
// Exercise 88: ES6 Class - Basic Usage
class Person {
  constructor(name, age) {
    this.name = name;
    this.age = age;
  }
  greet() {
    console.log(`Hello, I'm ${this.name} and
I'm ${this.age} years old.`);
  }
}
const alice = new Person("Alice", 28);
alice.greet();
```

Class Inheritance

```javascript
// Exercise 89: Class Inheritance
class Student extends Person {
  constructor(name, age, grade) {
    super(name, age);
    this.grade = grade;
  }
  study() {
    console.log(`${this.name} is studying for
grade ${this.grade}.`);
  }
}
const bob = new Student("Bob", 20, "A");
bob.greet();
bob.study();
```

Singleton Pattern

```javascript
// Exercise 90: Singleton Pattern
const ConfigSingleton = (function() {
  let instance;
  function createInstance() {
    return { apiUrl:
"https://api.example.com", timeout: 5000 };
```

```
      }
    return {
      getInstance() {
        if (!instance) instance =
createInstance();
        return instance;
      }
    };
})();
const config1 = ConfigSingleton.getInstance();
const config2 = ConfigSingleton.getInstance();
console.log("Singleton instances same?",
config1 === config2);
```

Factory Pattern

```
// Exercise 91: Factory Pattern
function createCar(make, model) {
  return {
    make,
    model,
    drive() {
      console.log(`${make} ${model} is
driving.`);
    }
  };
}
const car1 = createCar("Toyota", "Corolla");
car1.drive();
```

Observer Pattern

```
// Exercise 92: Observer Pattern
class Subject {
  constructor() { this.observers = []; }
  subscribe(observer) {
this.observers.push(observer); }
  unsubscribe(observer) { this.observers =
this.observers.filter(obs => obs !==
observer); }
```

```javascript
  notify(data) {
this.observers.forEach(observer =>
observer.update(data)); }
}
class Observer {
  constructor(name) { this.name = name; }
  update(data) { console.log(`${this.name}
received: ${data}`); }
}
const subject = new Subject();
const observer1 = new Observer("Observer 1");
const observer2 = new Observer("Observer 2");
subject.subscribe(observer1);
subject.subscribe(observer2);
subject.notify("New Event Occurred");
```

Debugging, Testing, & Best Practices

Console Logging for Debugging

```javascript
// Exercise 93: Console Logging for Debugging
function calculateSum(a, b) {
  console.log("Calculating sum of", a, "and",
b);
  const sum = a + b;
  console.log("Result:", sum);
  return sum;
}
calculateSum(5, 7);
```

Using the debugger Statement

```javascript
// Exercise 94: Using the debugger Statement
for (let i = 1; i <= 3; i++) {
  debugger; // Use browser dev tools to
inspect 'i'
  console.log("Iteration:", i);
}
```

Try/Catch for Error Handling

```
// Exercise 95: Try/Catch for Error Handling
function parseJSON(jsonStr) {
  try {
    return JSON.parse(jsonStr);
  } catch (error) {
    console.error("Parsing error occurred:",
error.message);
    return {};
  }
}
console.log(parseJSON('{"name": "Alice"}'));
console.log(parseJSON("invalid json"));
```

Custom Assertion Function

```
// Exercise 96: Custom Assertion Function
function assertEqual(actual, expected,
testName) {
  if (actual === expected) {
    console.log(`PASSED [${testName}]`);
  } else {
    console.error(`FAILED [${testName}]:
Expected "${expected}", but got "${actual}"`);
  }
}
function add(a, b) { return a + b; }
assertEqual(add(2, 3), 5, "add() should return
sum of two numbers");
assertEqual(add(2, 3), 6, "add() intentional
failure test");
```

Testing Asynchronous Code

```
// Exercise 97: Testing Asynchronous Code
function asyncAdd(a, b, callback) {
  setTimeout(() => {
    callback(a + b);
  }, 500);
}
```

```
asyncAdd(4, 5, (result) => {
  assertEqual(result, 9, "asyncAdd() should
return correct sum");
});
```

ESLint Configuration (Conceptual – as comment)
```
// Exercise 98: ESLint Configuration
(Conceptual)
// An ESLint configuration file (e.g.,
.eslintrc.json) sets rules for code style and
error detection.
// For example, enforce 2-space indentation,
single quotes, and semicolons:
/*
  {
    "env": { "browser": true, "es6": true },
    "extends": "eslint:recommended",
    "rules": {
      "indent": ["error", 2],
      "quotes": ["error", "single"],
      "semi": ["error", "always"]
    }
  }
*/
```

Debounce Implementation
```
// Exercise 99: Debounce Implementation
function debounce(func, delay) {
  let timeoutId;
  return function(...args) {
    clearTimeout(timeoutId);
    timeoutId = setTimeout(() =>
func.apply(this, args), delay);
  };
}
// Test debounce with a simple log function:
const debouncedLog = debounce((msg) =>
console.log("Debounced:", msg), 300);
```

```
debouncedLog("Hello");
```

Throttle Implementation
```
// Exercise 100: Throttle Implementation
function throttle(func, limit) { let
inThrottle; return function(...args) { if
(!inThrottle) { func.apply(this, args);
inThrottle = true; setTimeout(() => inThrottle
= false, limit); } }; } // Test throttle by
logging scroll positions (simulate with a loop
here) const throttledLog = throttle(() =>
console.log("Throttled log"), 1000); for (let
i = 0; i < 5; i++) { throttledLog(); }
```

This comprehensive set of exercises (with complete code)
should help you practice and master JavaScript—from basics
to advanced topics. You can experiment further by modifying
and combining these exercises to create more complex
projects.

Conclusion

As you reach the end of this JavaScript Crash Course, take a moment to reflect on the journey you've completed. Throughout this book, you've explored the fundamental building blocks of JavaScript — from understanding basic syntax and control structures to mastering advanced topics like asynchronous programming and DOM manipulation. Each chapter was designed not only to teach you the technical aspects of coding but also to encourage you to think critically and solve real-world problems.

By working through the interactive exercises, quizzes, and mini projects, you've built a strong foundation that will serve you well as you continue your programming journey. Remember that coding is a continuous learning process: every challenge you encounter is an opportunity to improve your skills, experiment with new techniques, and ultimately become a better developer.

As you move forward, keep these best practices in mind:

- **Code Regularly:** Consistent practice is essential to reinforcing what you've learned.
- **Experiment Freely:** Tinker with the examples and create your own projects.
- **Review and Reflect:** Use feedback and errors as stepping stones to improvement.
- **Stay Curious:** JavaScript is ever-evolving; maintain your hunger for learning and innovation.

Your journey doesn't end here. Use this course as a stepping stone to dive deeper into more advanced topics, explore popular frameworks, and contribute to real-world projects. Embrace every challenge with confidence, knowing that your newfound skills empower you to create dynamic, interactive web experiences.

About the Author

Laurence Lars Svekis is a distinguished web developer, educator, and best-selling author with a deep passion for JavaScript and modern web development. With over two decades of experience in front-end and full-stack development, he has dedicated his career to teaching and empowering aspiring developers through hands-on exercises, real-world projects, and interactive learning resources.

Laurence is widely recognized for his expertise in JavaScript, guiding learners from fundamental programming concepts to advanced topics such as DOM manipulation, asynchronous programming, API integration, and modern JavaScript frameworks. His teaching approach breaks down complex topics into digestible, step-by-step explanations, making JavaScript more accessible for beginners while offering advanced techniques for experienced developers.

Through his best-selling books, online courses, and live workshops, Laurence has helped over a million students worldwide master JavaScript and build dynamic, responsive web applications. His practical coding challenges, project-based lessons, and in-depth tutorials ensure learners gain the hands-on experience necessary to confidently apply JavaScript in real-world scenarios.

Beyond education, Laurence actively contributes to the JavaScript and web development community by sharing open-source projects, creating innovative learning tools, and engaging in discussions on the latest advancements in JavaScript and web technologies. His commitment to continuous learning and improving the developer experience has made him a trusted mentor and authority in the industry.

To explore more of Laurence's work, access additional learning materials, and connect with him, visit BaseScripts.com.

Thank you for joining this JavaScript Crash Course. May your coding journey be filled with curiosity, creativity, and continuous growth.